THE COMPLETE GUIDEBOOK TO
OPTIMUM BODY ENERGY

ACHIEVE YOUR POTENTIAL
BUILD YOUR STRENGTH
MAXIMIZE YOUR DURABILITY

DORI LUNESKI R.N., N. D.

authorHOUSE®

AuthorHouse™
1663 Liberty Drive
Bloomington, IN 47403
www.authorhouse.com
Phone: 1-800-839-8640

The information contained in THE COMPLETE GUIDEBOOK TO OPTIMUM BODY ENERGY is intended for health education only and may not be construed as medical advice or instruction. The information is not intended as a substitute for advice, supervision, or direction from your physician or other health care provider. No action should be taken based solely on the information in this manual. The reader should consult with his or her health care professional on any matter relating to his or her health and well-being. Readers who fail to consult with appropriate health care professionals assume the risk of any complications from the health education provided. The information is received from sources believed to be accurate, but is not intended to diagnose, treat or cure any disease.

Published by AuthorHouse 5/17/2012

ISBN: 978-1-4685-4752-8 (sc)
ISBN: 978-1-4685-4751-1 (e)

ACKNOWLEDGEMENTS

To ...

Eddie Archuleta for his unending support of my projects. He excels as a business manager for HM Wellness Center LLC.

To ...

Dan Luneski whose talent helped design the front and back covers. His artistry is apparent in everything he does. He is an asset to the HM Wellness Center LLC team.

To ...

Patrice Luneski PhD Holistic Nutrition who was instrumental in improving the content and editing of this manual. She is also invaluable as a member of the HM Wellness Center LLC team.

TABLE OF CONTENTS

'How To' Build Your Energy Manual 1

Exercise ... The Energy Booster 5

Body pH Balance Gives You Energy 7

Water Gives You Energy 9

You Have More Energy When Protected from Polluted Frequencies 11

Organic Food Gives You Energy 13

Healthy Brain Function Gives You Energy 15

Energy from Sleep 17

More Tips for Sleep That Gives You Energy 19

Cold or Flu Symptoms Cause Loss of Energy 23

Constipation Can Cause Loss of Energy 25

Diarrhea Can Cause Loss of Energy 27

Pain Can Cause Loss of Energy 29

Maintaining Your Energy with Restaurant Food 31

Prevent Energy Loss Even with a Cut or Burn 33

You Can Lose Energy with Germs in the Mouth 35

The Energy Benefits of Probiotics 37

Even Carbon Dioxide Gives You Energy 39

How Do You Trust the Word 'Organic?' 41

You Can Lose Energy with Old Mercury Fillings 43

You Can Lose Energy with Root Canals 47

When You Alkalize ... You Energize!!! 51

Your Goal Should Be the Prevention of Disease 53

Build Energy on a Cellular Level 55

Energy Healing 59

Chronic Fatigue Is Big Time Energy Loss 63

Energy Is Priceless!!! 65

Energy Loss from Simple Mineral Deficiencies 67

Flouridation Can Cause Energy Loss 71

When the Germs Win You Lose Energy 73

Energize Your Circulatory System 75

Energy Comes from Correct Calcium Balance 77

Increase Your Energy with Stress Management 79

Energy Loss from Dust Mites 83

Energy Loss from Chemicals …Surviving Pesticides 85

Energy Loss from Contaminated Food 87

Energy from Natural Food Supplements 89

The Energy of Homeopathy 93

Homeopathic Sources for Vital Energy 95

The Energy of Bach Flower Remedies 97

The Energy of Color 99

Renew Energy with Proper Grieving Process 101

Energy Is the Fountain of Youth 105

A Strong Immune System Supports Energy 107

An Autoimmune Disease Robs You of Energy 109

The Most Important Energy Lesson to Learn 111

HOLISTIC COOKBOOK

Introduction to Healthy Meal Planning 115

How to Make a Quick Fabulous Salad 117

Cooked Vegetables Add Spark to a Meal 119

    Carrot Recipes 119

    String Beans or Asparagus 119

    Broccoli, Cauliflower, Asparagus, Zucchini or Green Beans 120

Chicken or Vegetarian Rice Bake 121

Hot Salmon (or Vegetable) Buns 123

Ostrich, Buffalo, Turkey Bacon, or Vegan Sandwich 125

A Healthy Version of Seafood or Vegan Pasta 127

Grilled Vegetables 129

Fabulous Macaroni Chicken Dinner 131

Healthy Sausage 133

The Healthy Hot Dog 135

Ideas for Breakfast 137

Ways to Fix the Incredible, Edible Egg 139

    Scrambled Eggs 139

    Egg Omelets 139

    Hard Cooked Eggs 140

    Deviled Eggs 141

    Egg Substitutes 141

Healthy Treats 143

Easy Soup Ideas 145

Dessert Recipes 147

    Pumpkin Pudding 147

Pecan Sauce 147

Pumpkin Pie 148

Grapefruit Sorbet 148

Six Ways to Enjoy Left Over Chicken 149

Scotch Broth 151

Bouillabaisse 153

Chicken or Turkey Oregano 155

Don't Forget About Black Eyed Peas 157

My Favorite Black Eyed Peas Recipe 157

Marinated Black Eyed Peas 157

Quick Butter Bean Soup 159

Clam, Salmon, or Corn Fritters 161

Hope for Pizza and Macaroni Cheese Lovers 163

Quesadillas 167

Chicken Paprika 169

Chicken or Turkey Pilaf 171

Meat or Vegetarian Hash 173

Baked Fish and Rosemary Potatoes 175

Clam Stuffed Mushrooms 176

Rosemary Chicken 177

A Simple Meat or Vegetarian Casserole 179

Great Sauces Over Drop Biscuits 181

Side Dish Vegetables 183

Greek Oven Fries 183

Mashed Cauliflower 184

Delicata Squash 184

Brussels Sprouts 185

Green Beans 185

Other Vegetables Too Many People Ignore 186

The Forgotten Vegetables 187

Chicken with Dumplings or Noodles 189

Dumplings 190

The World's Healthiest Legumes 191

Pantry/Refrigerator Soup 193

Awesome Meatloaf 195

Do You Love White Potatoes? 197

Fabulous Stew 199

Awesome Macaroni Salad 201

Bean Stew 205

Nutritional Blender Drink 207

Beans and Rice 211

Grilled Fish and Vegetables...213
Fish Sticks, Pasta and Quinoa Salads...217
    Fish Sticks Made at Home 217
    Pasta Vinaigrette with Artichoke Hearts.................................218
    Do Not Forget About Quinoa for Easy to Digest Protein........218
Additional Ideas for Basic Ingredients...219

'HOW TO' BUILD YOUR ENERGY MANUAL

If what you are doing is working for you, then you are one of the fortunate few. But if what you are doing is not working for you **then this manual will help you WANT to make changes** while eliminating some of the challenges that occur while you are "re-energizing" your life.

For just a minute try to think how it would feel to have all your needs and wants met. Are you *completely* content with your ...

- future security?
- contribution to mankind?
- completion of personal goals?
- personal image?
- professional image?
- personal health?
- attitude about life's challenges?
- level of **energy** to get you through the day?

Are you interested in a life change because ...

- pieces are missing from your life puzzle?
- your life puzzle is finished and you do not like the picture?
- you are existing in a pattern of survival?
- you've never taken the time to REALLY evaluate all the situations in your life?
- you just plain need an attitude adjustment?
- you are sick and tired of being sick and tired?

Do you understand what stressors drive you?

- Ambition can be striving for success.
- Storms can be family and relationship concerns or illness.
- Self indulging and instant gratification can be "I" oriented instead of "We".
- Procrastination can be putting off what needs to be done now.

Robert Schuller said, *"If you get where you're going, where will you be?"* Frustration is the internal conflict between *what we have become*, and *the way we would like to see ourselves*. Being overworked and constantly stressed without enjoying rewards makes too many people exist in a state of delusion. If you are in *a survival mode* due to unresolved frustrations that leads to negative mental attitudes, the most intellectual, successful, financially comfortable professional can live his/her life *as a victim in a choking state of stress.*

These few lines are from a book preface written by James Kavanaugh. *"A shocking part of society has turned downright vicious and struggling for survival in a dog-eat-dog world. Some people do not have to search for life's meaning. They find their niche early in life and rest there, seemingly content with their world. There are, however, millions of people who are not unhappy, but neither are they really content. They behave like survivors, but a part of themselves got lost in the struggle."*

You may have thought, "been there, done that", when life is presented with disappointments. A high quality of life can be summed up in just a few words. It means that the person has enough **ENERGY** on all levels of mental, emotional, and physical to keep **IN** the "discomfort zone" that allows reasonable risks for personal, professional, and spiritual growth. If you don't wake up every morning a little nervous about what you are doing, you are not stretching yourself. The positive interpretation of that "nervous" feeling produces an exhilarating high that says THIS DAY IS NOT LIKE ALL THE OTHERS. That clear intention to remain spiritually, mentally, and physically active produces the body chemistry that allows us to remain vigorous as we age. Instead, too many people survive each day with multiple discomforts, or go from doctor to doctor, drug to drug, or collapse into bed glad the day is over.

Our life journey should not be to live longer, but to have enough ***comfortable health and bountiful energy*** to enjoy life as we age. *Although infant mortality and even life expectancy has improved, <u>has the quality of life improved?</u>* We need to look at the increase in cancer wards for adults and children, new dialysis hospitals being constructed, increase in degenerative brain disorders, chronic fatigue and depression, low motivation, obesity and diabetes, divorce statistics, criminal activity statistics, chronic and acute illnesses that could fill a book to determine if we are <u>**really**</u> in control of "wellness" in this country. *We need to look at the health of our children to get an idea where we are headed in the future.*

The next time you evaluate your success, do not just look at your possessions and bank account. Success itself should not be a goal … it should be a life's journey that must include the quality of your health. A rubber band has no value until it is stretched. That may sound like a cliché, but before you tune it out, take a second to give *your life a real hard look.* Are you really the best you can be … the healthiest you can be … or are you content in either *your comfort zone … or your discomfort zone?*

Dr. Viscott M.D. and author of "RISKING" states …

> *"Not risking is the surest way of losing. You never learn who you are, never test your potential, and never stretch yourself. You become comfortable with fewer and fewer experiences. Your world shrinks and you become rigid."*

I want to assist a progressive thinking person to walk through the door to a better understanding of his/her personal needs, personal growth, and energy management. Your professional career, your personal life, and your dedication to health and a sense of energetic well-being should be a balance … working in harmony with each other. What you experience each day is the best day of your life. Too often by mid-life we regret that the life we led was not a rehearsal! It is never too late to challenge yourself to new and exciting horizons. Albert Einstein said, *"Insanity is when you do the same thing every day and expect a different response."*

Continue on reading each exciting page if you are ready to be the best you can be! Continue on reading each exciting page if you want to prevent disease instead of having to treat disease! Continue on reading each exciting page if you want to be in control of your healthy body, instead of your unhealthy body controlling the quality of your life! You are not alone … Dori Luneski, Naturopathic Practitioner is with you all the way!

Let's turn the page together …

EXERCISE ... THE ENERGY BOOSTER

THE FIRST WEALTH IS HEALTH ... Ralph Waldo Emerson

You are starting one of the most important segments of your life journey ... *control over all of who you are on all levels of spiritual, mental, emotional, and physical.* You will receive the guidance needed to assist you in making your journey easy and successful with the information in this manual, and also from my book *"The Power to Heal"* (there is an Exercise Chapter). I suggest you read one "energy tip" and one "recipe" each day, to slowly and collectively accumulate *a treasure of information that will give you a lifetime of health benefits.*

Today the energy tip you include in your **EVERYDAY** plan is exercise that moves the *lymphatic system ... your Doctor within that cleans up toxic wastes.* It is your lymphatic system that cleans the blood, and that means 30 minutes **MINIMUM 6-7 days a week nonstop.** You might get away with 6 days a week, but you will not get enough health benefits from 5 or less days a week. Consider any choice that impacts the bottom of the feet, like walking, trampoline, treadmill, etc. It is NOT recommended that you jog or run at this stage since you may not be hydrated with enough water, and that can be hard on the joints that are all cushioned with water. ***ABOUT 30 MINUTES OF WALKING TYPE EXERCISE 6-7 DAYS A WEEK THE REST OF YOUR LIFE IS A MUST IF YOU WANT TO ENJOY "FEEL GOOD ENERGY" AND SURVIVE LIVING IN MODERN AMERICA!*** During part of the walk, give thanks for all the special people, opportunities and blessings in your life. **Use this private time to focus on your blessings to increase energy and _not_ what is missing to deplete energy.**

"The dog ate my homework", is nothing compared to the excuses I've heard for not having time to do this important health recommendation. My personal plan for **total compliance** starts when I get up, go to the bathroom, drink a glass of water, take my probiotic good bacteria on an empty stomach, and start walking for 30 minutes fast through the rooms on the 1st floor of my home. I walk with 3-pound weights to build upper body strength, deep breathe to push all the air out of the lungs, and thank God with a big smile for the gift of life this day, for the sunny day or rain that is the miracle of life. If you cannot do 30 minutes, at least do 10 minutes and increase as tolerated while you develop your "habit". If you cannot walk, consider a balance ball, or rocking chair allowing your **bare** feet to impact the floor

or carpet as you bounce or rock. **BEGIN THE DAY WITH ENERGY THAT WILL BENEFIT YOU ALL DAY!**

One lawyer solved his time problem by setting a timer, and marching in his office while reading his briefs. Another lady never had a break once she got to her office. She solved her problem by parking further away, so it took her 30 minutes to get to her office door. Another lady never had a spare minute once her children got up, so she waited until after breakfast and the youngest children were amused watching her exercise to music with the older ones. *Trying means nothing … when it comes to exercise, you either do, or you don't. You get no physical health credit for critically needed energy with only wishful thinking! Figure out what fits your lifestyle and MAKE IT HAPPEN DAILY!* **Smile and have an energetic day … and make someone looking at you also feel better.**

BODY PH BALANCE GIVES YOU ENERGY

School children get their school supplies before school starts, and since you are in your own version of the "school of life", you also need supplies. Along with daily exercise, you get energy improving your urine and saliva pH. THE BASIC CAUSE OF DISEASE IS AN IMBALANCE IN THE BODY CHEMISTRY. **That means you need pH testing paper**. One source is 1-718-338-3618, or www.microessentiallab.com. All pH testing paper is the same ... it tests pH of whatever liquid you are testing. Some products are more expensive than others because they read other values besides pH, like in diabetic testing supplies. All you need is the least expensive paper that tests the broadest range for easier reading. The pH paper used to test swimming pools or fish tanks is not calibrated fine enough for human data.

All filtered water is dead water, and needs to be energized with electrolyte minerals like organic sodium. NO HEALTH EFFORT WILL BE AS SUCCESSFUL USING THE BEST <u>FILTERED</u> WATER, WITHOUT <u>REPLACING</u> THE **MINERALS** LOST IN FILTRATION. One mineral replacement suggestion is pH Plus from Essential Water and Air, 1-800-964-4303, or www.ewater.com, or from HM Wellness Center. Another product that restores water to its original pure state is Bio Vitale from Longevity Formulas, 1-800-285-4116, or from HM Wellness Center. Bio Vitale contains iodine as an antioxidant so it may not be tolerated by people with Hyperthyroid. Some bottled water companies are now adding minerals back into the water, so look for those choices.

You cannot digest food to regenerate cells, make hormones that mellow you, or enzymes that keep you alive if your saliva pH is too acid or too alkaline. Saliva reading for digestion of 6.6 is low normal, and at 7.4 you are too alkaline to digest protein correctly. Urine reading under 6.6 suggests you are not handling stress well. Above 7.0 you are losing alkaline minerals, so you may want to adjust your diet from fruits and vegetables to include more grains and protein, reduce the pH drops in your water to no more than 4 drops per quart. You should also evaluate if you are consuming too many alkaline supplements from alkaline based foods. A health professional or manager of the supplement section of your health food store can help you if you are not sure.

These health tips are not intended to teach you all you need to know about this subject, but should introduce you to important health information you can learn more about. *I talk about pH in the Digestion Chapter of "The Power to Heal"*. Without correct pH you may not get the value of expensive supplements or organic food, as much as you think you should from the effort you are making. **THE PH OF YOUR URINE OR SALIVA TELLS YOU IF WHAT YOU ARE DOING IS WORKING FOR YOU . . . OR NOT . . . SO PAY ATTENTION TO THIS IMPORTANT AND INFORMATIVE BODY LANGUAGE!**

So, you now understand the importance of nonstop walking type exercise at least 30 minutes 6-7 days a week for lymphatic drainage You appreciate the miracle of life, and you are ready to order supplies for pH testing. **CONGRATULATIONS ... YOU ARE THE MIRACLE OF THE MOMENT BUILDING ENERGY THAT MAKES LIFE ENJOYABLE!**

WATER GIVES YOU ENERGY

You are **not ready** for your exciting journey if you do not have all your 'healthy' ducks in a row. You know the importance of exercise, and have purchased your pH testing paper. You have an energizing solution for all filtered water you drink. **That's good!** Today you need to think about a critical element of health protection … **a healthy drinking water source. That source should be easily available in your home. You should not have to run to the grocery store if you are out of safe water. *That makes it likely you will either substitute unsafe water, or drink less than you should to stretch what you have.*** Gary A. Martin DSc., PhD. states, *"The water you are drinking contains someone's disease marker. The quality of your water should be your #1 health concern."*

Water deserves top billing where health is concerned. Dehydration is the **number one stressor** of the human body, or of any living matter … try not watering your plants and see what happens. **Water controls free movement of molecules, so exchange of nutrients and elimination of toxins can occur.**

We are composed of 70 % water, 85% in the brain cells. Water volume in your spinal discs supports 75% of the weight of your upper body. Cartilage in joints and discs are 50% water. *The digestive system is ineffective without correct water.* Symptoms or pain anywhere in the body can be a sign of local cellular thirst. **Everyone who comes to my office with any symptom has dehydration as part of the problem!** Some people have cellular dehydration because they flush everything out from over hydration. *Too much of a good thing does not make it better.* **Your daily energy depends on correct hydration based on 1 ounce for every 2 pounds of body weight … unless you are a Hydripheric Type (overweight) discussed in my book "*The Power to Heal*."**

Our industrial society has severely compromised our water with high levels of inorganic minerals, toxins, heavy metals, chemicals, and drugs. Too often we do not understand that the lack of the most important element in the human body … healthy energized water … can clog any system or organ, and generate pain and illness. Small filters may only take out chlorine and some heavy metals. Distilled water has no molecular energy; is very acidic; and can flush out good nutrients. You should test well water for arsenic. Unless you have a reverse osmosis or other high quality system for drinking water, I suggest you temporarily order a reputable home delivery service of **filtered spring water** that has been **ozonated for parasites.** *Do not order filtered city water.* Also purchase a shower filter for city water, because you breathe in chlorine from the steam and absorb 60% of what goes on your skin. Have your house water tested to make sure it is not too acidic that can corrode your pipes and cause financial stress.

MAKE THE WATER YOU DRINK THE BEST IT CAN BE! Lately, even hard plastic containers are controversial, so to be safe, carry water in stainless steel or glass; carry plastic bottles that are BPA free and do not have a plain #7 on the bottom. *Add energizing mineral drops to **ALL** filtered drinking water!* ***Carry energized drinking water with you wherever you go ... shopping, restaurant, or to work.*** **THIS IS YOUR LIFE... IT IS NOT A REHEARSAL!** With your health education developing daily, you can learn how to take care of your body ... ***so when you get where you are going, your energetic body will be there with you.***

YOU HAVE MORE ENERGY WHEN PROTECTED FROM POLLUTED FREQUENCIES

Now it is time to get to a serious health problem. In the last 50 years we have become a society of polluted frequencies that will change the world forever. We now live in a world that is dominated by electrical equipment and products, polluted frequencies from computers, power lines, cells phone, beepers, microwaves, oversized TVs, and children obsessed with electronic games. We also live in a world of angry and frustrated people that impact the health of people around them with vibrations from negative emotions. Your body uses internal energy ***BORROWED FROM NORMAL BODY FUNCTION*** to protect you from all polluted, scrambling frequencies. *Too often, the exposure exceeds your ability to protect you from these invading frequencies.* ***At the very minimum, energy needed for that protection is borrowed from normal body function keeping some other important functions from getting the energy they need!!!***

Fortunately, our technology has also produced ways to divert those negative frequencies away from you. The BioElectric Shield (available from my office) will deflect all negative frequencies; check www.bioelectricshield.com/HMWellnessLLC for information. One day my BioElectric shield was being energized in the window at home. I went to a computer store to purchase a faster computer, and forgot to put my shield on. The whole store was full of computers and TV programs running. Without the shield, I was shocked how my concentration diminished, my pulse raced, and I felt dizzy and nauseated. I needed to stay and make a decision about the purchase, so I borrowed my husband's shield. In only a few minutes my pulse slowed down, and I felt able to think clearly again. **That was a dramatic reality check about life with modern technology!**

An additional preventative healthcare tool is Tachyon Technology that is a MUST have protection for cell phones, digital cordless phones, computers, television, electronic equipment and games. *This is not a substitute for the BioElectric shield that has broader protection,* **but extra protection, since an unprotected cell phone is like talking with your head in a microwave, and cordless phones are potentially even more dangerous.** For more information check www.tachyon-partners.com/hmwellness, or call 301-865-9600 and talk to Eddie. **DO NOT LET POLLUTED FREQUENCIES ROB YOU OR YOUR FAMILY OF VALUABLE HEALTH PROMOTING ENERGY.**

What is stress? One explanation is the opposing reaction of a body resisting a force. That force in modern American is different than any other time in the history of the world. We can no longer maintain the body energy we need for normal body function when we must struggle daily, even hourly to resist so many negative frequencies that are foreign to the body. **Protecting yourself with products that _deflect_ negative frequencies is not just recommended in modern times, IT PROTECTS THE QUALITY OF LIFE AND CAN BE LIFE SAVING. Tachyon Technology has many products that help retain our energy for normal body function!!!**

This health tip is really big!!!!! You are beginning to get a picture of *how to survive living in modern America. **Hope you will soon have an unscrambled day.***

ORGANIC FOOD GIVES YOU ENERGY

Now it is time to go shopping for food. You do not have to throw out hundreds of dollars of food, but you should know that you can improve your energy through your **correct choice of new food purchases**. The typical American diet is disease producing. We must stop pouring chemicals into our bodies with herbicides, pesticides, and fungicides in chemically raised produce, hormones and antibiotics in animal products, and a multitude of chemicals in processed and refined food. The EPA has registered over 900 pesticides, and they are in over 20,000 products we are using. Many herbicides, fungicides, and pesticides have been found to be carcinogenic. *Given our current health statistics consuming **organic** food, unless you are out socially, is a no brainer!!!*

The most difficult part of any dietary change is a person's ATTITUDE. The key to dietary change is *emphasizing* how many delicious and healthy foods are available … *NOT* what you have to give up! Because you *choose to be healthy*, you can *choose to reduce consumption of unhealthy choices*, find acceptable substitutes when possible, and treat yourself occasionally to foods you miss socially. How you react to those foods will determine how 'social' you are willing to be. The reward for dietary changes may be the energy you are seeking. Do not set yourself up to feel frustrated because you WANT something you now know is not good for you. **Once you start to feel better and have more energy, you will realize the importance of <u>eating to live, rather than living to eat.</u>** *Trust me; I was seriously ill for 20 years, so being healthy is a real kick!!!!* I travel a lot, eat out at least one time a week, and enjoy my birthday cake (that I sometimes make organic at home). The difference is that I am **SELECTIVE** of what I eat out … and **what I eat at home is always organic or all natural!!!**

Nutrition is not the whole health story, but it is something for which there is no substitute. Check the recipe section at the end of this manual to help set up your 'new kitchen.' An organic diet sets up the process of building health and energy. Commercial food can be grown with only water and added nitrogen, potassium, and phosphorus. The rest of the minerals can be missing, as well as many trace minerals, and added chemicals produce toxic wastes that can be disease producing or carcinogenic.

I do not eat dairy products, beef, deep fried, processed food, or soy products that are high in estrogen look-a-likes. I occasionally eat organic buffalo, lamb, duck, or turkey bacon; refined sugar limited to special occasions. Chicken, turkey and eggs are hormone and antibiotic free, and I order ocean fish or seafood in a restaurant (no farm raised fish unless there is no better choice on the menu). I eat ocean or ecologically farm raised fish at home; no alcohol or caffeine; organic fruit occasionally; non-dairy rice milk. My cheese needs are met with Manchego sheep cheese and Water Buffalo mozzarella; also sheep yogurt. Of course, lots of organic vegetables, organic nuts and seeds, organic <u>sprouted</u> whole grains including super digestible gluten free Quinoa and Teff, and low glycemic index sugars like Coconut Secret products. ***I was 78 on February 3rd 2012 and look many years younger, with a 5 foot 2 inch frame that stays slim. I have energy that lasts all day, a desire to be in service to mankind, and a joyful enthusiasm for life ... you decide what you want to eat.***

HEALTHY BRAIN FUNCTION GIVES YOU ENERGY

So you want to remember everything you are learning. Good luck unless you know some healthy brain tips. Our society is in epidemic levels of short and long term memory loss. Alzheimer's disease and senile dementia are starting earlier than ever before, plus shocking statistics for heart disease, and male sexual concerns. **What is happening to our circulatory system?** *Dehydration is a big part of the problem, and 85% of the brain is water. We must look at the use of billions of chemicals, prescription and nonprescription drugs.* However, major causes of circulatory change are far from common knowledge ... ***triglycerides, pre-diabetes or diabetes***. The typical American diet can produce triglycerides, causing plaque formation anywhere in the circulatory system ... the brain ... the heart ... the male sexual organs. *Stopping this run-a-way train is easy if you understand the foods that produce triglycerides ... when eaten in excess.*

Remember the word EXCESS. I am not suggesting total elimination, but these foods clearly need to be consumed in minimum amounts to control triglycerides. **The single most important thing you can do to keep your brain functioning at its peak, and prevent brain aging, is to be vigilant about what you eat and drink.**

1. Red meat should be antibiotic and hormone free. Beef can be allergic, is generally poorly digested, and in a restaurant is most likely not hormone and antibiotic free. Both beef and pork are high in bad fat, and slow down stomach digestion hours longer, causing other foods to ferment. *Good fat is where it's at ... as far as brain health is concerned.* This is a reversal of the fat phobia Americans are caught up in eliminating **all fat** from their diet. If we do not eat the right kind of fats ... <u>**essential fatty acids**</u> ... the brain suffers. Degeneration and disease is the long term result. *So much for refined foods!!!*

2. Alcohol in excess converts to triglycerides, so keep your drinks to one socially ... *and try not to be social everyday.*

3. 'Fruitaholics' can produce triglycerides. One serving of organic fruit daily does not mean a huge fruit blender drink every morning with equivalent to 3-6 servings of fruit. My Father did that and died of his 4th heart attack at age 56.

4. *Fruit juice has become America's water but does not count as water,* so it adds to our

shocking long list of chronic and acute health problems. Fruit juice may contain high levels of mold, since they only juice secondary fruits. The fruits that are lowest in mold are organic pineapple, grapefruit, mango, papaya, and pure pomegranate. Make sure you wash the outside of fruit very well before cutting. All fruit contains fructose but tropical fruits are highest in fructose. It is best to limit fruit to one time a day of American grown fruits (apples, berries, pears, etc.)

5. Refined sugar is in so many refined foods! Read ingredients and try to reduce this hidden or not so hidden troublemaker. Even natural sugar and fruit feeds cancer. Fructose in large amounts can convert to triglycerides. Use low glycemic index sugars like Stevia or Coconut Secret Crystals or Coconut Nectar.

6. Refined grains are a big part of the typical American diet obsessed with <u>delicious</u> and not <u>nutritious</u>. Look for organic pastas like Tinkyada and <u>sprouted</u> whole grain breads. **A metamorphosis … the new 'you' is beginning to emerge.**

ENERGY FROM SLEEP

You are learning some **basic "laws" of wellness** with exercise, pH of body chemistry, healthy water, protection from polluted frequencies, some healthy diet tips, healthy brain function *so you can remember it all* ... **and now it is time to go to sleep.**

The circadian rhythm for healing occurs between 8 PM and 4AM when people in past generations used to sleep. You can only heal and regenerate during deep REM (Rapid Eye Movement) sleep. Electricity and technology of modern times discourages most people from getting enough REM sleep to slow the aging process. Going to bed by 10 PM is best, 11 PM is fair. **You should get a minimum of 4 ½ hours of sleep before 4 AM.** Do not drink any water 2 -3 hours before going to bed, except a small amount if needed for bedtime products. ***Do not stay in bed more than 8 hours, or you will lose calcium needed to balance pH.***

The quality of your bed can make a huge difference in restful sleep. *Use only natural fiber bedding and sleepwear.* A typical 'chemical' mattress is made primarily from crude oil and natural gas derivatives: polyurethane, Styrofoam, polyester, dyes, fire retardants and a host of other chemicals. Polyurethane foam, as an example, is made from a number of ingredients that are recognized carcinogens. **New 'technologically advanced' chemical bedding and sleepwear is a health disaster!!!!** *No wonder our immune system is so wiped out, since it gets so little rest at night.* **I suggest you cover your mattress and your pillow with an organic barrier cloth cover you can order from 1-800-Janices, or other natural product catalogs.**

OH NO! Dust mites live in pillows, mattresses, duvets and blankets where they lay their eggs and multiply, being fed by a constant supply of dead skin cells off your body ... another reason for barrier cloth covers on your mattress and pillows. The tiny mite droppings are made airborne by our slightest movement in bed. It is when the allergen is airborne that it can be harmful. When the allergen is inhaled or comes into contact with your skin, symptoms like asthma, eczema and other related allergic conditions can be triggered. Sooooooo ... *you do not have to tell me twice to shower or bathe at night with a good brisk rub-down to get rid of skin cells that gives mites dinner; plus wash my sheets weekly, and the rest of the bedding monthly.* Once a month you should put your pillow in the freezer for 12 hours and in the dryer for 30 minutes to eliminate mold, mites and dust. **Protecting the immune system from working all night is top priority as you try to survive all the stresses of living in modern America!**

If you snore, you ... *or anyone near you* ...cannot sleep deep enough for healing. You will not snore if you breathe through your nose. But, if your sinus is blocked, you will breathe through your mouth … **and snore.** The answer is very simple for 95% of my clients. *Use a good nose spray with two sprays in each nose, sniffing hard after each spray, then sniffing hard through both nostrils and blow if needed. This must be done three times a day until snoring stops.* The spray I use in my practice is Xlear, available in some health food stores, 1-877-599-5327, or www.xlear.com.

Good night … and if you still cannot sleep, there are more suggestions on page 19.

MORE TIPS FOR SLEEP THAT GIVES YOU ENERGY

So what do you do if you can't zzzzzzzzzzzzzzzzzzzzzzzzz? Most people do not go to bed when it gets dark, or get up with the chickens anymore. Remember, you should get a minimum of 4 ½ -5 hours of sleep by 4 AM. *If you have trouble getting to sleep, or staying asleep, these health tips may help:*

1. **DO NOT NAP DURING THE DAY.** You may feel refreshed, but it could make it harder to get to sleep, or stay asleep during the healing cycle at night. You should always look for the reason you cannot stay awake all day. Saying, 'I enjoy my nap' is not a good enough reason.

2. **EXERCISE DAILY.** The simple truth is you need to make your body tired enough to want to sleep. Exercise moves the toxic wastes out of your body that interferes with healthy body function. Isometric exercises flex and hold muscles for a short period of time to help leverage the relaxation impulse… try this:

    i.   Lie on your back, inhale through your nose and exhale slowly … **continue this throughout the routine.**

    ii. Tense your toes tightly for a count of 10 … relax.

    iii. Tense your calves, count to 10 … relax. Continue to tense for a count of 10, and relax each of the following: thighs, buttocks, stomach, hands, arms, shoulders, neck, and face.

    iv. Finally tighten all muscles for a count of 10 and relax. Repeat routine if you are not relaxed enough to sleep.

3. **CHANGE YOUR DIET.** Sugary snacks before bedtime may at first give you energy, but when your blood sugar drops you get sleepy, and when it drops even lower during the night you wake up and cannot get back to sleep. Food allergies like milk or beef can wake you up during the night as your body starts to withdraw from the food. It is worth a try to consider food allergies as the early morning wake up call you would rather not have. Caffeine products may also have to be evaluated. Some people can

have sleep problems if they consume caffeine products in the late afternoon or into the evening.

4. **IMPROVE DIGESTION.** Read the Digestion Chapter in my book to allow your body to make hormones that control all bodily functions, including sleep hormones like Melatonin produced in the pineal gland. Remember, Melatonin is a hormone, and can be abused as a supplement. Nan Fuchs Ph.D. in her December 2005 WOMEN'S HEALTH LETTER stated it is generally considered safe up to 3 mg. Taking Melatonin in higher doses, with some prescription drugs, and some cancers should be evaluated and monitored by your doctor.

5. **DO NOT HAVE A LIGHT ON IN YOUR BEDROOM.** The night-light should be in the bathroom. Light in the bedroom stops Melatonin production.

6. **YOU NEED PLENTY OF BRIGHT FULL SPECTRUM LIGHT IF YOU ARE INDOORS MOST OF THE DAY.** These are not ordinary fluorescent bulbs, or regular light bulbs. Full spectrum lights mimic daylight that contributes to melatonin production you will need at night.

7. **WASH NATURAL FIBER BEDDING AND SLEEPWEAR BEFORE USING.** The formaldehyde sizing in 100% cotton needs to be washed out unless it says organic cotton, and will not wash out in perma-press cotton.

8. **SHOWER OR BATHE** after dinner to get rid of dead skin cells that feed dust mites, but also clear negative frequencies for more tranquil balance. There are calming herbal formulas that can be used in the bath water or as a shower gel for relaxation. If you are too tired to shower at bedtime, or if it wakes you up, then shower just before or after the evening meal.

9. **WASH SHEETS WEEKLY AND MATTRESS PAD MONTHLY.** Pillow cases should be changed more often, even nightly if you have mold sensitivities. Mold grows on your pillowcase in 24 hours.

10. **COMFORTABLE ROOM TEMPERATURE** should not be too hot or too cold, too few covers or too many, as an uncomfortable temperature interrupts sleep.

11. **CONSIDER SOFT MUSIC IN YOUR BEDROOM** while you are getting ready for bed. Listening to soothing music can help you sleep longer, wake up less frequently, and be more awake during the day. Buy a tape recorder that shuts off at the end of the tape. *Listen to music every night, and watch your sleep improve.*

12. **WEAR A BIOELECTRIC SHIELD** discussed on page 11 at night to protect you from electromagnetic frequencies if you live ½ mile from major power lines. Do not

sleep with a computer or TV on (best unplugged if not in use), or any other electrical appliance near your bed like electric clock (use battery clocks), charging base with cordless phones, or cell phone chargers. You can get Tachyon products that will protect you from using electrical equipment in the bedroom.

13. **TAKE THE RIGHT MINERALS AT BEDTIME.** Many people take calcium at bedtime, but that can actually contribute to anxiety, and cause muscles to contract. A better mineral to take is magnesium. Taking Magnesium Citrate powder at bedtime relieves anxiety and relaxes muscles. It also may increase bowel movements, so consider your history and elimination needs before taking Magnesium Citrate (available in most health food stores).

14. **KEEP PETS OFF THE BED** to reduce parasites and mites in the bedding, and not wake you up when you need your valuable anti-aging sleep … *sorry.* Pets can be trained, so you decide who is training who!!! I trained my cat not to get on the bed, and not to meow until I got up … honest!!!

15. **HOMEOPATHICS** sold in many health food stores, calm and encourage deep sleep with no morning hangovers. A good recommendation to start is Hyland's Calms and Insomnia. If needed you can also add Mag. Phos. cell salt and Chamomilla. Homeopathics are safe in any strength up to 30x every night without concern about addiction and are safe if you are on prescription drugs.

16. **CONSIDER AN HERBAL SEDATIVE** available in most health food stores in both tea blends, tablets or vegetarian capsules. Do not take herbal sedatives with over-the-counter or prescription drugs without checking with your doctor.

17. **BREAKING A BAD SLEEP PATTERN** can be difficult, but *reprogramming your subconscious every night that you <u>will</u> sleep better, instead of going to bed confirming that you never sleep well is a critical place to start.* Reprogramming the subconscious takes time, so do not give up just because you had your usual night. Do not get into the habit of staying up to read or watch TV if you cannot sleep. Stay in bed, do the relaxation technique, keep your eyes closed and at least rest. It can take months of doing everything right to break a bad sleep pattern.

GOODNIGHT *zzzzzzzzzzzzzzzzzz*

COLD OR FLU SYMPTOMS CAUSE LOSS OF ENERGY

This 'how to' list contains user friendly information everyone should know, but is not intended to replace medical attention if needed. The recommendations are easy to find products in most health food stores that may help moments when you feel *your energy is sinking into the sunset.* ***You want to have them on hand for the 'unexpected' at home or traveling.***

I'll use a personal experience as an example. On a recent cruise my husband and I got up *daily* about 6AM, toured islands all day, ate way too much including desserts, ballroom danced all evening getting to bed about 2AM. On the 4th day of this *very enjoyable insanity*, we had reservations in the special dining room with freezing air-conditioning where I sat. Wrapped in an alpaca shawl that is 50% warmer than wool, I still ended up in what seemed like hypothermia. I shivered my way back to our room, building a headache, sore throat, and body aches ... but ... Dr. Dori to the rescue to stop what could have messed up the rest of the cruise. *I'll list your emergency first aid routine.* If you follow the recommendations **AT THE FIRST SIGN OF SYMPTOMS,** you should never have your day ruined with *miserable symptoms:*

1. **AT THE FIRST SIGN** start thumping your sternum (breastbone) with four fingers for 15 seconds, at the top of the breastbone just below the hole in your neck. Behind the sternum is your **Thymus immune system** gland that controls inflammatory problems. Repeat every 30 minutes until you are symptom free.

2. **AT THE FIRST SIGN** take an **Adrenal immune booster** product of choice that you already purchased for unexpected stress (and always carry with you when you travel). My favorite is Cytozyme AD (never tests allergic) from Biotics Research 3 x day; available in most health food stores. You might also purchase other herbal **liquid** products (not capsules), Homeopathic or **vegetarian** products to boost the adrenals.

3. **AT THE FIRST SIGN** take **Garlitrin 4000** from PhytoPharmica 1-2 x day, available in most health food stores. *The garlic comes in individual foil, so I always keep foil wrapped garlic in my change purse ready for the 1st sign of cold, chilling or aching.*

4. **AT THE FIRST SIGN** take your favorite **antioxidant formula**. My favorite is

Lipoic Acid, a universal antioxidant that works throughout the body. I recommend Solgar brand, available in most health food stores, and take 120 or 200 mg. up to 4 times a day.

5. **AT THE FIRST SIGN** of aching, take ½ tube of **Oscillococcinum** by Boiron, under the tongue; available in most health food stores and some pharmacies. It is a big word that does a big job when needed; repeat ½ tube in 6 hours. I always carry one tube with me in my change purse, *because you never know when the symptoms will start.*

6. **AT THE FIRST SIGN** take **Ferrum Phos. cell salt**, available in most health food stores. You should never travel without this tissue salt that carries oxygen – your first line of defense against bacteria or virus; and a healthy way to deal with fevers and inflammation. Take with **Mag. Phos. cell salt** for pain anywhere. You can take 3 pellets of each under the tongue every 15 minutes for acute symptoms; if possible purchase homeopathic remedies in a 30X strength … and reduce or eliminate when better.

7. **AT THE FIRST SIGN WALK!!!** Your **lymphatic system** is your doctor within. If we did not have a system that would protect us against invading organisms, then civilization would have died out a long time ago. Hundreds of my clients have told me how quickly they got over beginning symptoms by walking 30 minutes nonstop 2-3 times the day the symptoms started. If you have no products with you, it is possible to abort a cold or flu with Thymus tapping, water, and walking to let the lymphatic nodes clean up the toxicity.

8. **TAKE RESPONSIBILITY for WHY you got symptoms!!!** *The bad cold fairy did not hit you in the head,* so **IT IS TIME FOR A WELLNESS REALITY CHECK!!!**

CONSTIPATION CAN CAUSE LOSS OF ENERGY

This clearly is no fun!!! Besides the discomfort, you can get very tired from retaining toxic wastes, your skin can break out, headaches often occur, and you hesitate to put more food in when nothing is coming out. Your stomach bloats, body odor increases … *well, you get the picture.* Here are some user friendly recommendations that are **not intended to replace medical attention if needed:**

1. **The NUMBER ONE cause of constipation is *NOT ENOUGH WATER!!!***

2. **The NUMBER TWO cause of constipation is *NOT ENOUGH EXERCISE!!!***

3. **The NUMBER THREE cause of constipation is *pH IMBALANCE!!!***

4. **The NUMBER FOUR cause of constipation is *NOT ENOUGH GOOD BACTERIA,* and increased microorganisms like Candida Yeast or parasites.**

5. **The NUMBER FIVE cause of constipation is *POOR STRESS MANAGEMENT.*** Read the Positive Thinking Chapter in *"The Power to Heal."*

Americans are quick to turn to laxatives, but that can be addictive. There are many herbal laxative formulas in health food stores that support the whole digestive-intestinal interrelated system. Swiss Kriss is one that is gentle and easy to take when you travel. I recommend non-laxative favorites that help most people.

1. **Magnesium citrate powder** is available in most health food stores. Magnesium is always low when constipated, and should be the *1ˢᵗ line of defense to improve the problem.* Take ½ -1- 1 rounded scoop at night in water, or even hot water if the problem is severe … *relief is in sight!* If you travel, measure out a scoop for each night you will be gone, instead of taking the whole bottle with you.

2. Some people need more help, so consider adding anywhere from ½ -1- 1 rounded teaspoon of **Solgar Calcium Ascorbate Vitamin C powder** to the Magnesium Citrate powder. This combination taken at bedtime can produce great results.

3. Most people forget the obvious … **DRINK MORE WATER!**

4. Most people forget the obvious … **DAILY EXERCISE!**

5. Most people do not know what their **pH balance** is, so they do not know if their bowel is out of balance. Get your pH paper and test yourself.

6. Most people with constipation are low in **good bowel bacteria**. *Your best friend could be a dairy free probiotic supplement. Take 2 daily ½ hour before breakfast, LIFETIME!* This is especially important if you have old mercury fillings in your mouth, as mercury kills the good bacteria needed for a healthy bowel.

This short page of information is not intended to duplicate the **Elimination Chapter** in *"The Power to Heal."* That is a must read chapter since all disease includes retention of toxic wastes. *You will not get away with ignoring constipation.* **DO NOT BE SATISFIED WITH LESS ELIMINATION THAN IS NEEDED TO PROTECT YOUR LIFE!!!** *GREAT … WHAT DOES THAT MEAN?* **THAT MEANS A LARGE MOVEMENT BEFORE NOON, AND 1-2 SMALLER ONES DURING THE DAY** (sorry … reading material in the bathroom should not be necessary).

DIARRHEA CAN CAUSE LOSS OF ENERGY

Oh no … the 'D' word that strikes fear in all of us. People 'think' it is OK to live with constipation **(wrong),** but it is not possible to tune out diarrhea. You may need to seek medical attention, but you may be able to improve the condition yourself if you know the CAUSE, whether you are at home or traveling.

1. **Stress induced diarrhea from poor digestion or anxiety.**

   - Check pH of urine saliva and keep in the range of 6.6-7.0.
   - Add an extra glass of energized water for loss of fluid.
   - Evaluate the **Bach Flower Remedy test** in *"The Power to Heal"* and
   - read Chapter 1 on Positive Thinking **MULTIPLE TIMES!**
   - Health food stores carry many homeopathic calming, or stress related products, such as formulas that contain Ignatia, Valerian, Aconite, Phosphorus, Pulsatillia, Gelsemium, or Arsenicum album. *Formulas rather than single remedies may be more helpful.*

2. **Food intolerance.**

   - Big offenders besides allergy to dairy and beef, is a problem with the digestion of the milk sugar that can cause diarrhea.
   - Big gluten grain offenders include wheat, oats, rye, barley, and spelt. For best digestion eat only organic **sprouted** grains.

3. **Overgrowth of microorganisms like Candida yeast or parasites.**

   - This is discussed in the *"The Power to Heal"* Elimination Chapter.

4. **Mold from foods consumed.**

   - Eliminate cheese, leftover food; store unused bread in the freezer. All juice can have mold, because they do not juice 1st grade fruit.

5. **Bacteria or virus from immune suppression.**

- Chills, aching all over, or fever may give you a clue this is the problem.
- The bacteria or virus is *NOT YOUR PROBLEM*. **Your suppressed immune system *IS YOUR PROBLEM.***
- Consider Homeopathic Colloidal Silver (available at HM Wellness Center that does not contain mercury), liquid herbal immune boosters and antioxidants 3 x day until better (liquids are better than pills or capsules with diarrhea), and **Homeopathic formulas for diarrhea.**

6. **Over hydration flushes out good bacteria and the tissue cell salts.**

- Consider 3 pellets of all 12 Bioplasma tissue cell salts every 15-30 minutes until diarrhea stops, then 3 x day x 1 month, then consider these energizing tissue cell salts 2 x day lifetime. For cramping, consider Mag. Phos. 6X every 15-30 minutes until better.
- Replace good bacteria with probiotics that need refrigeration, but when traveling use Florastor probiotics that do not need refrigeration.

This is a tip that can save you from embarrassment! *For out of the country traveling, always carry a few maximum incontinent pads that could save the planned activity of the day. At home or in a restaurant* the best foods for diarrhea are cooked carrots, white chicken meat, millet, brown or white rice. *Don't you feel more in control?*

PAIN CAN CAUSE LOSS OF ENERGY

These recommendations are not intended to treat. *When in doubt, contact your medical doctor, or go to the nearest emergency room.* **In a less acute situation, these recommendations may provide total relief, or at least lessen the discomfort until you can get a holistic medical evaluation.**

1. **For acute chest pain and/or shortness of breath**, *it is safest to call 911.*

2. **For right lower quadrant pain in your abdomen**, lay flat on the floor, and press deep in the area, letting up quickly. If the rebounding effect produces severe pain, you may have an acute appendix, *so get to an emergency room quickly.*

3. **If the pain causes cramps or hiccups**, take 3 Mag. Phos. cell salts 6X up to 30X under the tongue every 15 minutes until relieved (available in health food stores).

4. **If the pain is from an injury**, there is nothing better than Arnica taken every hour if needed until you get relief, or get medical attention. Homeopathic formulas are better than single remedies, so look for formulas that contain Arnica. *Arnica works well with Ledum 30X for swelling due to injuries or surgery.* Other products for injuries available in health food stores include Traumeel or Topricin. 70% DMSO (not the 99% unless you want to smell like ripe garlic) is like a crème magnet **that improves circulation to get toxic wastes out and nutrition in … and that relieves pain.** If you cannot find 70% call 1-800-367-6935. Put DMSO on first for best results … that helps to carry any other injury cream you use.

5. **If pain is a headache**, a Reflexology book acquaints you with pressure points that help you understand the 'organ' source of the pain. Try Mag. Phos cell salts every 15 minutes until you feel better. Keep a diary for patterns that help you find the CAUSE of your headaches … before or after meals … associated with female cycles … increased stress related … sleep deprivation … mold exposure.

6. **If pain is a migraine**, understand 1st that a migraine is the straw that broke the camels back. *Unlayering some of the building blocks to the migraine is your 1st line of defense.* Stop generally allergic foods like milk and beef, wheat, or soy; drink energized water; walk

daily; move your bowels if constipated; control your interpretation of the stress in your life (Chapter 1 in *"The Power to Heal"*); eat organic food (*chemicals can contribute to pain or disease anywhere!!!*). **Get the picture … clean up the LIST of problems and the migraines may be controlled.**

7. **Sinus pain** may be from bacteria from root canals; mercury from old mercury filling; chemicals; or uncontrolled exposure to mold, dust, and danders. Keep the sinus open (and stop snoring) with 2 sprays of Xlear in each nostril, sniffing hard after each spray 3 x day. Xlear is in most health food stores or call 877-599-5327.

8. **MSM** (Methylsulfonylmethane) is very anti-inflammatory in high doses. Take up to 12,000 mg. daily for acute muscle or joint pain. At that level, **pure powder** is easier than pills, so check with your health food store.

9. *Pain anywhere can be a sign of local thirst.* **ARE YOU DRINKING YOUR ENERGIZED WATER WITH ADDED ELECTROLYES??**

10. *Pain anywhere can be a sign that your lymphatic system is backed up.* **ARE YOU DOING 30 MINUTES WALKING TYPE EXERCISE EVERYDAY??**

A few products **ON HAND** and a little knowledge can make a challenging health day a lot easier.

MAINTAINING YOUR ENERGY WITH RESTAURANT FOOD

This clearly depends on whether you are having an occasional celebration like a birthday or anniversary, or you eat out a lot, or are traveling for a week or longer. The 1st rule is not to order foods you know will make you sick. *Some guidelines are:*

1. **NEVER** order animal products with hormones and antibiotics unless it is a rare special event. I never order beef or dairy products, pork, turkey, chicken, or eggs. Only order farm raised fish if there is no other choice, otherwise order ocean fish.

2. **NEVER** order anything deep fried, as the oil is most likely rancid, since they either only change the oil weekly, or just strain and add more oil.

3. **NEVER** drink city water from the restaurant. You should be carrying energized water with you so you can drink ½-1 glass before you eat. If you do not have water with you, ask for non-carbonated bottled water. **NEVER** order carbonated water, as that leeches out calcium that you need to balance pH. *Restaurant ice has been tested and can contain bacteria, so ask for an empty glass with no ice and pour in your own healthy water.*

4. **NEVER** drink hot liquids with your meal as it WILL interfere with enzyme activity. So, skip the hot tea. I won't even discuss coffee ... OK I will. Coffee dehydrates, is acidic and over stimulates the pancreas, liver, and adrenals that are **TRYING TO DIGEST AND PROCESS YOUR MEAL ... THE FOOD THAT KEEPS YOU ALIVE!!!** *Don't mess with Mother Nature.*

5. **NEVER** drink alcohol with your meal as it enlarges the pores of the intestines letting undigested food and wastes go through, **making your liver mad at you.** Just because some people, even whole countries take alcohol with their meals, does not make it healthy. *Our life expectancy statistics suggests we are doing A LOT WRONG!!!* Read the Digestion Chapter in *"The Power to Heal."*

6. After a full meal, **NEVER** order a sweet dessert that will just mess up digestion. You can take it home to enjoy it in a relaxed environment several hours later.

7. **So what do I order in a restaurant that does not energetically wipe me out:**

   – Buffalo, lamb, duck, Cornish Hen may be free of hormones/antibiotics.
   – Ocean fish (ask if it is farm raised, like salmon, trout, catfish, or Tilapia).
   – I order shell fish if there is not a good ocean fish on the menu. Crab is better than shrimp because crab comes from the claw or legs of the crab, and does not have the intestinal vein like shrimp.
   – Salad with non-dairy dressing; and ask for **NO** head lettuce that is very chemical and low in nutrition (ask for dark leaf or Spring mix).
   – If you have a grain allergy you MIGHT do better with white bread or pasta than whole grains in a restaurant because lower protein means less allergic reaction. Ask for real butter and not margarine.
   – Olive oil and garlic, or tomato based sauces instead of creamy sauces.
   – Rice over potatoes, since commercial potatoes are full of chemicals!

You should eat organic at home, and order the best you can during your *'night out', trip or vacation*. Adhering to **strict dietary protocol** will not make you healthy if you get upset about feeling deprived at a special occasion. **Enjoy your life … but be reasonable in your selections!**

PREVENT ENERGY LOSS EVEN WITH A CUT OR BURN

Some cuts may need stitches, and some burns may need medical attention, some insect bites and rashes itch like crazy. For the usual crisis, there are three products that should be in every home in America. *The 1ˢᵗ is Thunder Ridge Emu Oil. <u>It is truly the product that heals.</u>* I first came across this product at a health fair, and was impressed at the pictures of a person with a severely burned face, and the incredible healing without scars that was on the 6 month photos. *I could list many personal and professional testimonials, but I'll limit it to three:*

1. A 3ʳᵈ degree burn on my thumb from a restaurant sizzling hot plate blistered right away. I hurried home and applied Emu Oil, and in 15 minutes the burning stopped. I applied the oil several more times before going to bed. By morning the blister went down, and I healed quickly without broken skin.

2. I got a steam burn across all my knuckles lifting a lid off a pan, and again the oil stopped the pain, and it healed without blistering.

3. I got a deep cut on my finger from a new sharp knife, and considered going to the emergency room for stitches. I decided to try Emu Oil and a very tight band aide. The bleeding stopped, and by bedtime I was able to use more Emu Oil, plus a looser band aid. In the morning the cut was sealed enough so I did not have to put on another band aid. The cut healed without a scar.

Emu oil can be used for everything from dry skin to insect bites, or a burning rectum. **Pure Emu Oil** is rich in essential fatty acids; and has anti-inflammatory, moisturizing, anti-aging and healing properties which expedite recovery. It has been used successfully on stiff swollen joints, burns, cuts, and chronic skin conditions. Since it is loaded with antioxidants and slows down the aging process, it has become the latest Hollywood craze for cosmetic miracles. *This is first-aid peace of mind!* I was a speaker at the 2008 Emu Association National Convention (*How many people do you know can say that?*). I was impressed at the numerous medical doctor speakers showing slide documentation of the healing power of Emu. You can obtain details on their line of products at 1-703-631-9074, or ThunderRidgeEmu.com; also available at H.M. Wellness Center LLC. Emu skin products should be refrigerated when not being used daily.

The 2nd unique product is **Super PAV** made from tree-resin, olive oil and food grade petrolatum (not chemical). It is antibacterial, antifungal, and antiviral, for any skin condition. This three-fold anti-disease action, plus the healing and pain relieving characteristics of the resin, has resulted in an incredible track record and a renewed interest among health professionals as an Indian remedy that is natural, harmless and effective. Available at H.M. Wellness Center LLC or www.natrhealth.com. or 1-800-422-4716. This is a fabulous product to take on a trip for all those unexpected crisis situations; needs no refrigeration. Do not take if you have a pine allergy.

The 3rd superior product for all skin problems from bites, cuts, rashes, to burns is **DermaTox**, a mineral spray that works miracles. Order from the company 1-800-604-6766, or www.KinoTox.com.

Collect your 1st aid kit now!

YOU CAN LOSE ENERGY WITH GERMS IN THE MOUTH

"There are more germs in a diseased mouth than there are stars in the Milky Way." *Tooth Fitness*, Thomas Mcguire, DDS

Many people remember seeing relative's dentures in a glass of water. They were healthier with dentures than we are with root canals to save the teeth. If a root canal is recommended, I suggest you research it thoroughly with a holistic dentist before consenting to have one done. Taking care of your teeth and gums should be a prime focus in preventive medicine. *You cannot casually brush, occasionally floss, ignore regular dental cleaning, eat less sugar and hope for the best. So what does a person do?* The **Sonicare** sold in many stores, www.sonicare. com, or 1-800-682-7664, reduces bacterial bio-film and breaks up plaque that causes gums to bleed, and/or recede. Highly recommended to use <u>with</u> the *Sonicare* is the *Waterpik* that flushes the toxins out of the gums to prevent gum disease that can be the beginning of disease elsewhere in the body; add a little hydrogen peroxide at the end of the water. <u>*Most dentists recommend the 2 minute rule that is 30 seconds each front and back, top and bottom!!!*</u>

An excellent option to flossing is *The Doctor's Brush Picks* (available in most pharmacies) used before each brushing. Bacteria and virus cannot live in oxygen so consider putting hydrogen peroxide on your toothbrush before you apply the toothpaste. Cutting down on bacteria and viruses in the mouth can help prevent disease anywhere in the body. *In cleaning, some toothbrushes will dissolve in alcohol, but all with tolerate hydrogen peroxide.*

A super quality mouthwash can also perform miracles in your mouth!!! Mouthwash is often used to mask bad breath, when your real problems are poor digestion and elimination, *plus an unhappy liver.* Using a mouthwash sounds easy enough, but do you want to swish around synthetic colors, chemical oils, alcohol, and sweeteners in your mouth? Look for a mouthwash made from herbal extracts in most health food stores.

Have your teeth cleaned every 6 months, or every 3 months if you have a lot of stress or gum disease. Controlling the health of your teeth and gums is a critical part of controlling disease! **If you cannot control gum disease you are not controlling stress in your life from mental, emotional, physical, chemical, or polluted frequencies.**

- **The Natural Dentist Herbal Mouth & Gum Therapy Daily Oral Rinse** – found in drugstores and health food stores; clinically proven to kill bacteria in the mouth. The antibacterial qualities come from Echinacea, calendula, and grapefruit seed extract;

and bloodroot that is shown to reduce plaque and bleeding. If you cannot find it, call 1-800-615-6895. It is *expensive*, so I use a small amount in the cap that is less than recommended on the bottle.

— **Diluted Hydrogen Peroxide ½ with water swished in the mouth for 30 seconds is an inexpensive mouthwash and gargle for short term sore throats.** Rinse mouth after use to eliminate the foaming action.

NOW SMILE AND SHOW OFF THOSE HEALTHY TEETH AND GUMS!

THE ENERGY BENEFITS OF PROBIOTICS

THE ONLY WAY TO GOOD HEALTH IS THROUGH THE STOMACH.

Research has discovered that the one thing healthy people have in common is a high level of 'friendly' bacteria throughout their digestive system. Antibiotics given as prescription drugs, and antibiotics in food destroy this *friendly* intestinal micro-flora. Some of the other offenders that can deplete *friendly* flora are stress, alcohol, sugar, drugs, processed foods, tobacco smoke, estrogen, chlorinated tap water, even the aging process. The opposite of antibiotics that kill both illness causing bacteria **AND** friendly flora is probiotics which literally means 'promoting life'. Probiotics promote good digestion and other beneficial functions that make them essential to life. ***Most people do not understand the power of these tiny life savers in their search for wellness.***

In the early 1900's the probiotics theory by Russian Nobel Prize winner Elie Metchnikoff believed that the long life of Bulgarian peasants was the result of their daily consumption of fermented milk products. It is this lactobacillus acidophilus that points to the health and longevity of many cultures. Metchnikoff believed that the bacillus that fermented the milk positively influenced the *friendly* micro-flora of the colon, decreasing the toxic effects of *unfriendly* bacteria. <u>100 years ago we were not all allergic to milk</u>. Because of the daily challenged immune systems of most Americans and abuse of dairy products, I have not found one person in 15 years of testing on my biofeedback machine that was not allergic to milk on the allergic point. So, we need to get our *friendly* cultures from another source. We tend to have a society high in estrogen due to the estrogen look-a-likes in chemicals, and high use of soy that also has estrogen look-a-likes is not a good alternative. Commercial yogurt processing is not the same quality people use to eat, and may not have enough good bacteria to produce colony growth. To set up good colony growth of *friendly* bacteria, you need **strong probiotics taken on an empty stomach.**

What are just <u>some</u> of the energy benefits of probiotics?

- They provide the 'balance' to control all unwanted microorganisms, including parasites and Candida yeast that grow in the absence of healthy micro-flora.
- They normalize bowel movements to control both constipation and diarrhea.
- They stimulate the formation of antibodies to improve immune function.
- They create at least 7 essential B vitamins necessary for human health.

- They produce lactase to digest dairy products. People who cannot digest milk sugar are low in probiotics. This does not mean you should eat dairy, but you might not get diarrhea if you get dairy socially.
- They help regulate healthy energy in the entire digestive system controlling abnormalities in the intestines that prevents many skin disorders.
- They help regulate cholesterol levels in the blood.
- They help regulate hormone levels that can mellow your day.
- They help eliminate intestinal gas, bloating, and other signs of indigestion.

So run … do not walk to your health food store, and purchase the highest quality dairy and beef free broad spectrum probiotic supplement you can find. **YOUR WHOLE BODY WILL LOVE YOU FOR IT!!!**

EVEN CARBON DIOXIDE GIVES YOU ENERGY

We can live nearly 50 days without food, 5 days without water, but only 5 minutes without air. Most people know that breathing consists of inhaling oxygen **in** and exhaling carbon dioxide **out.** It is commonly believed that only oxygen is required for health and carbon dioxide is waste gas. The truth is we need **BOTH.**

If you light a fire, you would blow on it to give it oxygen; to put a fire out, you throw a blanket over it to keep oxygen from reaching the fire. Inside every cell in your body is the mitochondria that acts like a fire, and burns food to make energy. Most people's mitochondria lack the oxygen to function properly. Only 5% of your energy comes from the food you eat; 95% comes from enough oxygen. If there is not enough oxygen for the fire to burn properly, the fuel remains unused and energy cannot be made, so carbon dioxide levels are low. This unused fuel is stored in the body's fat cells. It is not just the food we consume that makes us fat and tired, *it is the food that we do not burn that makes us fat and tired*. When there is not enough oxygen to burn the fuel that we eat, the body makes lactic acid that stays in the body waiting for oxygen to turn it into energy. *One of the main causes of anxiety is elevated lactic acid levels from low oxygen.*

When oxygen is burned it makes water, carbon dioxide (CO_2) and energy. If you breathe quickly for 60 seconds you will become dizzy, and fingers and lips will start to tingle. That feeling is the carbon dioxide levels dropping . **Most people breathe far too fast for their own good. Rapid breathing brings in extra oxygen, but causes you to exhale too much carbon dioxide.** In order for oxygen to get into the cells it must be e*xchanged* for carbon dioxide. If there is not enough carbon dioxide in the blood stream, oxygen is forced to stay in the blood, and is never released into the tissues … so, a carbon dioxide deficiency makes oxygen deficient in the cells. *The following are 'good guy roles' played by carbon dioxide that …*

- makes your immune system stronger, faster, and able to recognize infections.
- regulates and protects proteins in your body by keeping them in balance.
- attaches thousands of hormones to carbon dioxide to keep things organized, but function ineffectively if attached to a sugar molecule.
- attaches neurotransmitters in the brain to carbon dioxide; but if they are attached to sugar, you cannot be as smart or as happy as you would like to be.
- protects digestive enzymes.

- prevents the nerve cells from being over stimulated.
- prevents muscles from cramping and hurting.
- prevents hyperactive brain activity like anxiety and insomnia.

The average person breathes twice as fast as they should, approximately 15 times a minute instead of the optimal rate of 8 times a minute. Faster breathing drops carbon dioxide levels causing **many stressors** that lowers your pH to be acidic, so if your pH is constantly acidic, check your breathing rate as a possible cause.

*So for health, **RELAXXXXXXX** to raise carbon dioxide levels. **You need to learn to slow your breathing rate, outside of exercise.*** This may take discipline to reset your body's natural, slower breathing rate.

HOW DO YOU TRUST THE WORD 'ORGANIC?'

You must first understand the problem to appreciate why organic food is a no-brainer! Organic food does not just eliminate herbicides, pesticides, and other dangerous chemicals proven by the EPA to be carcinogenic, but it also eliminates genetically engineered food. GE foods are engineered to tolerate heavier doses of chemicals. The first large-scale commercial harvest of GE crops in the US happened in 1996. By 1999, one-fourth of American crops were genetically engineered. Unlabelled GE foods now account for as much as two-thirds of all foods … and more are on the way. Since these foods have been rushed to the market so quickly, scientists remain in the dark about the long-term impacts of GE foods on our health. **Organic does mean it is <u>not</u> genetically engineered food, but a non-GMO (GE) label does <u>not</u> mean it is organic.**

The organic food industry is growing at a whopping 20% or more per year and many regular supermarkets now carry organic products. We use more chemicals in our food industry than any other country in the world, so imported food items from Europe may not state organic but may be raised with those standards. *Except for imported food or canned fish, every food item in my kitchen is certified organic or all natural.* The only time I eat non-organic food is in a restaurant. **These common titles you will see in different health food stores are all environmentally friendly, and include:**

- **USDA Certified Organic** means the land has not been treated with any toxic materials or chemical fertilizers for 3 years.

- **Local non-certified** usually comes from farmers who practice organic farming methods, but for meaningful reasons have chosen not to be certified.

- **Biologically Grown** produce is grown by developing the natural fertility of the soil, avoiding use of artificial fertilizers and chemical sprays.

- **Integrated Pest Management** (IPM) is socially acceptable, environmentally responsible, and economically practical crop protection. They resort to chemicals only if pests reach economically damaging levels.

Some chain health food stores intermingle organic produce with non-organic, and that is confusing to the shopper new to healthier eating. Some produce stockers may not always change the label when current deliveries change from organic to non-organic. You can only be sure it is organic if it has a certified organic label as a sticker or twisty. I prefer to shop at health food stores that only sell organic or environmentally friendly produce. *We are paying a huge price for fooling with Mother Nature.*

If scientists are experimenting through genetic engineering to grow fish at four times the natural rate ... what is the risk to you? Eat only ocean fish or seafood, not farm raised salmon, tilapia, trout, bluefish, rockfish, or catfish. Some health food stores sell ecologically safe farm raised fish and seafood. **We will have to take a hard look at a lot of our so called 'new and improved' ideas, to find a way to turn around the shocking health statistics in this country.** YOU CAN MAKE A BIG DIFFERENCE THROUGH YOUR PURCHASING CHOICES! MONEY TALKS IN THIS COUNTRY ... **AND YOU HAVE A VOICE ... BUY USDA CERTIFIED ORGANIC . . . OR ALL NATURAL!!!**

YOU CAN LOSE ENERGY WITH OLD MERCURY FILLINGS

Choose to be educated on the dangers of mercury fillings. There are references in my book *"The Power to Heal"* in the Resource References section. In his book "Whole Body Dentistry," Mark Breiner, DDS, states: "I now rank root canals right behind mercury amalgam fillings as a cause of ill health ..."

On September 6th, 2000 the Maryland Dental Board attempted to resuscitate its 'gag rule', requiring dentists to **falsely** tell their patients there are no 'legitimate' peer reviewed studies that link amalgam fillings to ill health. Such a rule supported bad science, help perpetuate unsafe-dental practices, violated our first amendment rights, and interfered with the consumer's right to be informed. In August 2000, the nonprofit consumer group DAMS and several citizens won a victory over this wrong-headed dental board policy when Judge Stuart Berger issued an injunction blocking the dental board's 'gag rule.' This and other cases changed the infringements on our health and freedom.

The current protocol for dental fillings is now ceramic and the current health trend discusses the removal of old mercury fillings. *It is however, very important that you go to a dentist who has been trained to take them out correctly and has up to date equipment that reduces your level of mercury absorption from the procedure. To find a dentist in your area that can do this procedure safely, connect with* www.holisticdental.org.

Taking mercury fillings out can be very costly, so how does a person protect their health until they can afford extensive dental work?

1. The most important place to start is to keep mercury **in your body MOVING!!!** That means drink your correct amount of ***ENERGIZED WATER EVERYDAY.***

2. Make sure you do **lymphatic walking type exercise at least 30 minutes minimum non-stop DAILY.**

3. Have a **good bowel movement** daily before noon, and preferably a second or third smaller movement during the day (*read the Elimination Chapter in my book*). Mercury is often the cause of constipation, and other intestinal disorders.

4. Consider **Solgar vegicaps Lipoic Acid** 120-200 mg 1, 3 x a day. Lipoic Acid is a universal antioxidant that protects all body cells from free radical damage.

5. Consider 100% herbal **CardioVital Plus** from Dr. Knoll Products, 1-800-877-2434. It is a potent blend of herbs and spices that make your natural cleansing agents go to work helping your body heal itself. Products like this can sometimes produce miraculous results, but should be discussed with your doctor for compatibility with other medications such as blood thinners. You must drink your correct amount of energized water and exercise daily to consider this product.

6. Make sure you take a **bath or shower every night** with a good brisk rub down to keep skin cells open. Mercury that comes out through the skin can cause boils, rashes, or itching. Use only organic products on the skin; avoid clogging oils, waxes, and products with perfumes and chemical additives.

7. An excellent book on mercury toxicity is *"It's All In Your Head – the Link Between Mercury Amalgams and Illness,"* by Dr. Hal A. Huggins. In 19 years of treating mercury toxicity Dr. Huggins has never been able to successfully treat mercury toxic patients on a vegetarian diet. There must be sufficient protein in the diet to stimulate the immune system. Test your saliva pH to help you understand the quality of your digestive system.

8. Avoid eating **a lot of larger fish, bottom feeder seafood, or seaweeds** that can be high in mercury. The fish lowest in mercury is Wild Planet sardines.

9. **Bowel Flora** products discussed on page 37 are critical to consider, since mercury kills *friendly* bacteria in the colon; **stay on daily probiotics lifetime.**

10. **L-Methionine** is an amino acid that suppresses and neutralizes toxic chemical activity, and functions as a chelator, a binding agent that deactivates and removes toxic substances by altering their molecular structure. *This product is A MUST CONSIDERATION to stay on as long as you have mercury in your mouth!* I recommend Pure Encapsulations vegicaps 375 mg. 2 x day empty stomach. Order from Emerson Ecologics, 1-800-654-4432, or check your health food store.

11. **Cilantro** herbal concentrate (available in most health food stores) can be used before or after amalgam removal to help release mercury from the tissues.

12. **Chlorella** (*Sun Chlorella is the best absorbed*), and algae like **Spirulina** bind with, and eliminate mercury. Check your health food store for products.

13. **DO NOT** use other *specific mercury detox products* until all mercury fillings have been removed, or you will pull mercury out of the fillings.

14. **Oxygen Spa Therapy** is a safe, effective method to aid in healing the body. Check your local health magazines (not the phone book) for licensed practitioners in

your area. Sweating toxins out through the skin can help with other toxins besides mercury. Understand that moving mercury can hurt, so if you are trying to cleanse the body of mercury, be aware that discomfort anywhere is possible.

15. **BioEnergiser D-tox Spa** starts the process of rebalancing your body's energy. Rebalancing the cells equilibrium of positive and negative ions 'kick starts' the dispersal of unwanted toxins. This highly recommended foot spa can be used at home to renew physical and mental energy levels, with a general feeling of well being. For more information contact www.gaiam.com, or call 1-800-869-3603.

A study at the Uppsala University Medical School in Sweden reported chronically ill patients contained abnormal levels of mercury in their cells. **Don't let heavy metal burden rob you of energy that will negatively influence your health!!!**

Articles like the one written by Jean Deardorff in the Chicago Tribune published December 11, 2005 states, *"Are your teeth toxic? The mercury in 'silver' fillings would be hazardous waste in a river … yet it's sitting in your mouth."*

There is help on the Web … consider these sites:
The American Dental Association: **www.ada.org.**
The International Academy of Oral Medicine & Toxicology: **www.iaomt.org.**
Consumers for Dental Choice: **www.toxicteeth.org.**
Institute for Biological Dentistry: www.ibdental.net

YOU CAN LOSE ENERGY WITH ROOT CANALS

Remember your grandparents dentures in a glass? We now have root canals, implants, gum surgery, crowns, braces, cavities filled, and antibiotics. Modern dentistry may be extremely helpful, but also may set you up for illnesses and diseases of the future. *We need to look at many of our medical and dental treatment choices to explain what might be causing the epidemic of degenerative conditions in this country.* Remember the quote from Mark Breiner, DDS in the previous health tip? The whole quote is, *"I now rank root canals right behind mercury amalgam fillings as a cause of ill health, and with an estimated 60 million root canals performed in 1998, you can appreciate the scope of the problem."*

WHAT DO YOU NEED TO KNOW ABOUT ROOT CANALS? During a root canal, the pulpal tissue in the tooth is removed, the canal sterilized and then packed to seal off the canal. A tooth's dentin (the material between the enamel and the canal) is comprised of millions of tubules to transport nutrients from the center of the tooth through the dentin to the enamel. It is not possible that these millions of tiny tubules (estimated they stretch 3 miles) can be sterilized during the procedure. With the canal sealed away from the cleansing and oxygenating effects of the blood supply, the bacteria left behind in the dentinal tubules begin to metabolize differently. *They change from aerobic (requiring oxygen) to anaerobic (without oxygen) to survive and become more toxic.* It is difficult to have a strong immune system in modern America, so the toxins enter your body as negative agents *and attack your weakest systems. The areas most often affected by root canal bacteria are the sinus, heart, breast and joints ... but root canal leaking bacteria can affect your body anywhere.*

If you have pain at a root canal site, I do not recommend having the dentist redo the root canal. Your immune system could be better off having it pulled and dealing with other options for the tooth. If you cannot afford to have root canals removed (*and they do not have to be infected to be suppressing your immune system*), then the following suggestions (**not intended to replace medical attention if needed**) will support your immune system and help control bacteria and viruses:

1. Drink your correct amount of **ENERGIZED WATER EVERYDAY.**

2. **EXERCISE** 30 minutes non-stop 1, 2, or 3 x a day based on your chronic symptoms and the number of root canals you have or pain at the site.

3. Have a **good bowel movement** every day before noon and preferably another 1-2 smaller movements.

4. Consider *Homeopathic* **Colloidal Silver** 3 x a day as long as you have any root canals. I do not recommend Colloidal Silver made at home or purchased in a health food store as you can accumulate silver if taken long term. The *Homeopathic* form is an energy factor, not the substance, and available from the Homeopathic sources listed on page 93.

5. Consider an **immune booster** product like we have discussed. There are many good **vegetarian, herbal, or Homeopathic** immune products in the health food store, so ask for help if needed.

6. Consider **Vitamin O,** worked up slowly to 30 drops 3 x a day. If you cannot find it, you can order from R Garden, 1-800-800-1927, or www.rgarden.com.

7. Consider **Lipoic Acid 120-200 mg. 3-4 times daily** based on symptoms and the number of root canals. Lipoic acid is a universal antioxidant that works in every cell in the body ... or consider any other **vegetarian or herbal** antioxidant product. **Seed-a-Sept** is a good antioxidant product from grapefruit seed, but may not be compatible with some prescription drugs.

8. **Thump your Thymus gland** as described on page 59. If you think you have increased sinus or respiratory inflammatory symptoms, you should thump your thymus every 30 minutes until feeling better. I thump my Thymus routinely 3-4 x day every day.

9. **Keep your sinus clear** so microorganisms have no food to multiply. Flush out your sinuses 3 times daily with Xlear nasal wash. If you cannot find it, order from 1-877-599-5327 or www.xlear.com.

10. **Make sure you get at least 4 hours of continuous deep sleep before 4 AM** to support the ability of the immune system to heal. You will not sleep deep if you snore, so use the Xlear nose spray 3 x day until snoring stops.

11. Take a **garlic** supplement daily, or 2 times a day if you are having pain at a root canal site, or have multiple root canals. My favorite is Garlitrin 4000.

12. **Eat organic, unrefined food!** The immune system already stressed from some root canals does not need the added stress of chemicals and processed foods that does not support the immune system.

13. **Purchase a toothbrush cleaning system** as discussed on 15. The vibrations break

up the bacterial bio-film that can be the breeding ground for bacterial inflammation anywhere.

14. **Purchase a BioEnergiser D-tox Spa** as discussed on page 45.

Before you get a root canal, think carefully about how the procedure might affect your <u>future health</u>. Root canals are 'big business', and you may not get all the facts if you ask a dentist who supports the procedure. Do your own research before considering a root canal!!! There are new procedures available that some professionals say improve the long term complications of some root canals. Sometimes 'new and improved' may be a breakthrough in the eyes of some professionals, but the person having the procedure is still a 'lab rat' for any 'new and improved' procedure or technique. If you already have one or more root canal, you'd better keep hydrated with energized water, protect your immune system with the 'laws' of wellness and natural food supplements and keep your lymph system moving with daily exercise!!!

Just like with mercury, check the websites on page 45 to help you understand the very controversial subject of root canals. If you do not have internet service, you can FAX the Institute for Biological Dentistry at 410-964-3154 for more information. The office number is 410-964-3118 if you cannot FAX.

WHEN YOU ALKALIZE … YOU ENERGIZE!!!

The reason disease is skyrocketing in spite of all our medical breakthroughs is simple … most people suffer from ACID OVERLOAD. *The typical American diet is acid-forming … meats, eggs, bread, milk and cheese, coffee, chocolate, sugar, rice, cereal, cookies, crackers, cakes, pies, candy, sugary drinks etc., etc., etc.* All that food we crave and love, added to over the counter and prescription drugs produces over-acidification of body fluids and tissues, and is linked in some way to **EVERY KNOWN DISEASE** including the ever popular fibromyalgia, chronic fatigue, digestive and elimination problems. *In the Sedona Health Letter Fall 2005 newsletter it stated "TUMS" is America's best selling drug.* To subscribe to this newsletter call 1-800-795-3080. *The pH story is in the Digestion Chapter of "The Power to Heal."*

A suggestion to alkalize saliva pH in a few days is with pure organic bottled lemon juice you can buy in health food stores. Take your probiotic first thing in the morning, and wait 30 minutes. Then take two tablespoons of lemon juice in any tolerated liquid like water or non-dairy milk, and wait 30 minutes to eat breakfast. Take two tablespoons 30 minutes after dinner, and again at bedtime. Reduce to one tablespoon, or take just one or two times a day **based on your pH or tolerance.** Lemon that is alkaline in digestion activates the pancreas to release sodium bicarbonate to alkalize the small intestine, urine and saliva. Adjust this recommendation based on your medical history and tolerance. If the lemon does not help your pH then the pancreas is *not* the cause of the acidity. Since lemon, beets, and olive helps the liver, you have supported that organ.

Nutritionists have discovered that 'green food' (**more** than green vegetables) lets you break the acid overload cycle. The nutritional wallop in 'green food' is fast becoming the food of the future. These modern miracle foods carry off acids, flush them through your kidneys and may be your 1st line of defense against fatigue, illness, and disease. Green is the color of healthy plants, new growth and healing … **and green foods keep giving seriously high nutrient levels squeezed into a ridiculously small space.** *It is called more bang for your buck!!!* **Here are 'super green food' facts:**

1. **Spirulina** is so complete in all the nutrients you could live off of just it and water. Some Spirulina has inconsistent control factors; *Earth Rise brand* is a good commercial brand. A **superior** source grown in controlled ponds is Organic Spirulina from Royal Body Care (a multi-level marketing company). This brand of Spirulina has a superior

delivery system. **If you cannot find a distributor for Royal Body Care,** call 1-800-722-0444 under my ID number 10984. *I want to make it clear I am **not** trying to build a business with this company. I recommend and use this high quality product myself because it is a **superior absorbed, organic super green food**.*

2. **Barley and Wheat Grass** (both <u>gluten grains</u>) have been promoted for decades for purifying the blood and detoxifying the liver.

3. The best brand for superior absorption of chlorella is **Sun Chlorella**, *a tiny dark green pill with the highest chlorophyll level of the green foods and screams out health just looking at it!!!* Remember, I'm super energetic at age 78; **I LOVE GREEN FOOD!**

YOUR GOAL SHOULD BE THE PREVENTION OF DISEASE

Breast cancer is now a major concern for women. Because of all the hormones in our animal products and exposure to look-a-like estrogens in foods and chemicals, men are getting breast cancer for the first time in history. We have a medical system doing technologically advanced research to cure diseases, ***but we are a society generally unaware of how to PREVENT diseases.*** According to the National Center for Health Statistics the top 3 causes of death in 1957 was Heart disease, Cancer, and Stroke. In 2007 the top 3 causes of death is the same order of Heart disease, Cancer, and Stroke. Currently, cancer is a serious concern for children and adults. **A few select principles of wellness can greatly improve anyone's risk factor.** *Consider the following PREVENTION rules that support the energy of health:*

1. 35 years ago I read an article that tight under wire bras prevented the proper flow of toxins and hormones from the breast, and contributed to the alarming breast cancer statistics. **So ladies, go down in cup size, up in bra size so it is not tight, and eliminate under wires (clip fabric and pull them out until you buy new bras).**

2. **Everyday drink your correct amount of energized, filtered water.** So you do not lose your water with dehydrating liquids eliminate or reduce caffeine except green tea.

3. **Everyday take a walking type exercise that impacts the bottom of the feet for 30 minutes continuously at least one time a day (2-3 times if you are sick).** Water and exercise moves the lymphatic system that cleans the blood.

4. **Have a good bowel elimination everyday before noon.** Bile acid that is not eliminated through bowel movements returns to the liver and reduces the amount of new bile acid the liver makes that day to eliminate excess hormones, chemicals, toxins from stress and poor digestion. If not properly eliminated, those toxins circulate through the system to destructive overload levels.

5. **WE MUST STOP THIS INSANE INGESTION OF HORMONES AND ANTIBIOTICS** in our animal products, fowl and farm raised fish.

6. **WHEN POSSIBLE BUY ORGANIC!** Non-organic fruits and vegetables can contain chemicals that have estrogen hormone look-a likes, and the body does not know the difference. Or look-a-like-estrogens can be high in some foods like soy; and a high animal fat diet can transform estrogen into the active form. In modern society with so many exposures acting in the body like estrogen, **organic soy is recommended in moderate use only.** Do not heat … carry food … or microwave (in soft plastic that converts to phenol-estrogens … **or microwave at all**). Carry food and water in stainless steel, glass, plastic other than plain #7 or Corning ware.

7. We need more nutrients than we can get from food to survive the stress of modern America. A **whole foods supplement provides phyto-nutrients from enzyme rich foods,** *and not just a list of nutrients made in a chemist's lab that has no synergy from one nutrient to the next, like food does. Chemically derived nutrients are not compatible with human chemistry in the same way as food.*

8. **Read the Elimination Chapter in *"The Power to Heal"* to control Candida yeast and parasites.**

9. Contact a holistic practitioner in your area for natural … and safer hormone needs.

10. **Mammography has proven not to be the best or safest way to evaluate breast health.** A current recommendation is Digital Infrared Thermal Imaging for the breast, or whole body for men and women. For more information check www.meditherm.com/breasthealth. *Carefully evaluate the REAL NEED for any diagnostic recommendations that uses radiation except in an emergency.*

11. **A PERSON'S ATTITUDE TOWARD LIFE IS A MAJOR PREDICTOR OF HEALTH … OR DISEASE!!!**

BUILD ENERGY ON A CELLULAR LEVEL

Every cell in your body is constantly a hotel for unwanted guests. The **energy producing factory** of each cell in your body is the mitochondria that has a private genetic code, separate from your overall genetic code. *The mitochondria provides 90% of the energy that fuels every cell in your body and keeps you alive.* **IT ALL FALLS BACK TO ENERGY!!!** When these energy producers begin to break down, so do the cells and organs. Protecting your mitochondria "power engines" from degenerative damage helps *slow aging at the very core.* The mitochondria DNA (genetic programming) is about 2,000 times more susceptible to damage from free radicals than your cellular DNA. In modern America the best way to protect your mitochondria is to slow the production of free radicals that damage it. *Consider the following:*

1. *"Eat less and live longer."* One of the effects of calorie restriction is to make the mitochondria more efficient and less stressed. These leaner, meaner mitochondria produce fewer free radicals as they generate energy than the over fed person next to you. **ALSO ... EAT ORGANIC!!!**

2. Consider **supplements derived from natural foods and herbs** and not made in some chemist's lab to *look like* a nutrient. *If God didn't make it, don't take it!* The best way to KNOW if the supplements you want to take are compatible with YOUR chemistry is to find someone with a biofeedback system similar to my SpectraVision. Or, purchase a book on Biokinesiology and teach someone to muscle test you. A compatible supplement will make you strong; an incompatible supplement weakens.

3. Consider boosting your **antioxidant defenses** with the following suggestions:

   – **Alpha Lipoic acid** is called the universal antioxidant. It is both water-soluble and fat-soluble, so it can pass through all cells to protect the mitochondria and other cellular components from free radicals. It can still function as an antioxidant even after it has donated an electron to stabilize free radicals. Most antioxidants are one-shot donors and are out of commission until another compound comes along to regenerate them ... but Alpha Lipoic acid **IS YOUR SUPERMAN** and becomes even more potent after giving up an electron. **This little wonder pill should be in everyone's wellness program.** It is available in vegetarian capsules and most health food stores carry 50mg. to 200 mg. capsules. In my office I have a 120 mg size from Solgar that is a good range to consider 1-3 times a day based on your general health, emotional and physical stress. In an acute inflammatory crisis or acute disease state, you should consider taking Lipoic Acid 3-4 x a day of a middle or high range strength.

— Another important player is **Coenzyme Q10** for energy production and free radical protection. ***COULD YOU USE MORE ENERGY? THE CENTRAL FAILURE IN HUMAN LIFE IS WEAKNESS ... LACK OF STRENGTH ... LACK OF PURPOSE ... LACK OF CHARACTER ... LACK OF WILL.*** Coenzyme Q10 is an essential component of our energy-generating system. *The energy demand of your heart, liver, kidney, pancreas, lungs, and muscles is especially vulnerable to CoQ10 depletion.* CoQ10 levels have been shown to be well below normal in patients with a wide variety of diseases. CoQ10 is an essential mitochondria nutrient that generates adenosine triphosphate (ATP) to activate intracellular energy. *There are many articles on the value of CoQ10, but unfortunately many commercial CoQ10 products do not test well on my biofeedback machine.* One brand I recommend is Vitaline CoQ10 from the health food store, or NEEDS Health and Wellness catalog 1-800-634-1380 or www.needs.com; or call Longevity Science 1-800-933-9440 for Advanced Q10.

— The final supplement for mitochondria protection is **L-Carnitine**. *If Alpha Lipoic acid is an engine-cleaning fuel additive and CoQ10 is a sparkplug, then Carnitine is the fuel pump.* Some of the most hard-working cells in your body depend on high-octane fatty acids as fuel, but they cannot enter the mitochondria without Carnitine as the carrier molecule that shuttles those energy rich nutrients across the mitochondria membrane. Most L-Carnitine is in beef capsules, but you can get the best grade I've tested from Longevity Science; consider 1 3x a day before meals. When you call, they would love to know Dr. Dori sent you. **Their products are all top quality, so ask for their product list.**

No anti-aging energy tip would be complete without reminding you of the 'laws' of wellness. If you have my book *"The Power to Heal"* you have a good beginning to understand what makes up the 'laws' of wellness. The typical American lifestyle and diet choices are aging people very fast.

In the last 50 years the changes we have made in technology is astonishing ... the decline in our 'health' is shocking. We may be living longer, but are we living healthier? In June 2007 AARP Bulletin states based on information from the National Center for Health Statistics that the life expectancy in 1907 for men was 45.6 years and for women 49.9 years. 100 years later in 2007 men improved to 75.5 years and women to 80.7 years, but obesity may cause American life expectancy to decline. At first glance it looks good, but a lot of that is because we improved our ability to deal with infection, accidents and life threatening situations. **With all our technology we should all be living a lot healthier without the need for so many drugs … and living a lot longer.** If you think we are living healthier in our senior years, ask some seniors how they feel and how many prescription drugs they are taking without any side effects; or visit a nursing home, an Alzheimer's unit, a cancer ward for adults and children or a kidney dialysis unit. **With all our technology in the last 50 years we have become a sick and diseased society struggling to survive in modern America. Children have become as chronically and acutely ill as adults. Our frustrations trying to attain the materialism of life have destroyed our values and too many people struggle daily in ways that reduce the quality of life. As a society we have become fragile.**

We have technologically advanced ourselves into disease and aging. We are no longer living the American dream … we are living the American nightmare! When you get where you are going … make sure your body can enjoy it! To survive in modern America and have any hope of controlling the aging process, you must take this book of energy tips as the most precious gift you have ever received. **ENJOY AGING GRACEFULLY!!!**

ENERGY HEALING

BY NOW YOU SHOULD KNOW HEALTH IS ALL ABOUT ENERGY!!! *Learning how to move your own **ENERGY** for increased health and vitality is the first step to wellness.* You can strengthen your immune system, improve circulation, cleanse the lymphatic system that cleanses you, and improve all body systems to provide energy for normal body function. Energy healing lays a sound foundation for the field of holistic medicine. *Any book on physics will tell you that energy cannot be destroyed, but it can travel and leave you weak as it leaves the body.* Contact healing, or acupressure, is a way of contacting the electrical centers in the body that show various areas in trouble when that pressure point is sore to the touch. Energy healing is not designed to diagnose or treat. *If you seek safer, simple, free methods of encouraging your body to heal itself then working **WITH** nature, and not **AGAINST** it may help you achieve health results.*

> *"ESSENTIAL FLOW OF ENERGY IS ESSENTIAL TO WELLNESS ... DISEASE IS THE RESULT OF ANY INTERFERENCE WITH THIS FLOW."* **Illya Prigogine (Nobel Prize Recipient)**

There are 12 main pathways of energy in the body called meridians. The Triple Warmer is the meridian that takes all the bumps, bruises and traumas to protect your body. *Unlike other meridians that relate to major organs, the Triple Warmer does not connect to any specific organ,* **but guards them all for optimum harmony and balance ...it is the immune system for the meridians.** Whenever something goes wrong with the energy of any organ, the first line of defense is to calm the Triple Warmer to keep it from taking over and weakening that organ as well as other organs in an attempt to rest the body. The Triple Warmer rests the body in case of a catastrophic stress like a poisonous bite, or any emotional or physical shock. *In modern America, we have polluted frequencies from power lines, computers, television, cell phone, beepers, microwaves, electronic equipment in our homes, cars and workplace. We are eating, breathing, wearing, and sleeping on chemicals that weaken our immune system. We have social, financial and career stresses. Modern drinking water is filtered dead water with no molecular energy, or we drink liquids we think is a substitute for water and either drink too much or not enough water. Juice and coffee has become America's water. Our food is too often nutritionally deficient and full of chemicals; and we often eat too much food with poor digestion. Taking prescription and non-prescription drugs, and having surgeries have become a way of life* *in modern America. We had none of this list 50 years ago!* **The Triple Warmer acts like it has to save us every day!!!**

When you need your Triple Warmer in case of body shock it will be there for you, but keeping your Triple Warmer calm in day by day living is your first consideration to protect your energy! This is a big part of learning how to survive living in the insane stress of modern America. I'll go over some points that **calm the Triple Warmer and support body energy and balance;** each should be done **at least** 2 times a day … during your morning exercise, and at night in the shower or bath. They can be done more often in acute situations.

- Place the thumbs on both sides of the temples (straight out from the eyes) just above where the side arms of glasses cross to the ear. Then put 3 fingers (from each hand) on the forehead going straight up from the top of the nose (like you are massaging a headache) … and massage **firmly** both the forehead and the temples at the same time 15-30 seconds.

- Place the thumb on the palm of the opposite hand for support, take 3 fingers and wrap them around the hand beneath the knuckles to **firmly** tap or massage the soft tissue **between** the bones of the little finger and ring finger for 15-30 seconds. If you have long fingernails, you can rub sideways in this soft tissue area.

- Take 3 fingers of one hand and **firmly** press the opposite temple just above the corner of the eye. **With a continuous firm push** move up over the ear, down right behind the ear, turn your head and continue down the neck muscle that pops up, then move over the top of the shoulder down the arm over the outside elbow bone. Without lifting any pressure from the finger tips firmly push the energy into the ring finger (next to your little finger) and without lifting your hand grab the whole finger to pull the energy out the end of the finger and throw it away. *Do not lift the pressure once you start the push.* Repeat 3-4 times each arm. **This is the Triple Warmer Meridian** and getting the energy out of the Triple Warmer so the working meridians work harder is best done with no clothes on. Getting the energy out of the Triple Warmer is your 1st line of defense if you feel wiped out or ill and need to get your energy back.

- The brain crosses over, with the left side of the brain energizing the right side and the right side energizing the left. *When the body is out of balance, the brain does not cross over causing loss of brain energy.* I'm sure you've heard someone say or thought to yourself, "I can't think well today." Encourage your brain to cross over by tapping your right hand to your left knee and your left hand to your right knee, 20 taps on each knee. Make sure you cross the arms over to tap the opposite knee and not just move them sideways. This will sharpen the brain … every time!

- **Firmly** tap your thymus (the inflammation control part of your immune system),

15-30 seconds at the **top of the breastbone** (the bone in the middle of the chest) with 4 fingers of either hand. You can tap the thymus **every 30 minutes to 1 hour** if you feel any inflammatory, cold or flu symptoms. You should be able to reduce or prevent these symptoms if you tap your thymus at least 3-6 times every day.

— Put your pointer fingers on the boney prominences at **both sides** of the hole in your neck, go down until you feel soft tissue on each side of the breastbone, and tap **firmly** with 3 fingers (top finger on the bone and two fingers under the bone in soft tissue) for 15-30 seconds. This is the 27th place on the kidney meridian that acts like a **whole body energizer** ... *think 'me Tarzan', and tap anytime you feel a loss of strength. This point will give you energy if you tap it 4-6 times every day. Think of it as your 'mother' meridian.*

— Tap 15-30 seconds ½ distance between the nipple of the breast and your side (on the rib cage) to energize the spleen, the largest organ of your lymphatic system. Tap more often along with the thymus if you have any inflammatory symptoms.

If you want training tapes and books on Energy Healing, contact Donna Eden at 1-800-835-8332, or www.innersource.net. **THIS KNOWLEDGE IS AN EXCITING ADDITION TO YOUR ENERGY HEALING AWARENESS!!!**

CHRONIC FATIGUE IS BIG TIME ENERGY LOSS

Fatigue is the #1 symptom most people complain about to their doctors. If you understand the causes of fatigue, your ENERGY level can be improved by your choices!!! *The major categories of fatigue are:*

- **Diet related fatigue** can be produced by blood sugar imbalances, food allergies, intolerances to the chemical composition of food, poor digestion, overgrowth of Candida yeast or parasites, nutritional deficiencies, chemicals in commercially raised food, or chemicals added to food ... ***EAT ORGANIC FOOD!!!***

- **Fatigue produced by other illnesses** such as cancer, poor kidney function, liver stress, anemia, sluggish thyroid, acute or chronic pain or depression.

- **Fatigue from 'side effects' of prescribed drugs.**

- **Fatigue from undiagnosed conditions (often referred to as Chronic Fatigue)** identified as a mixed infection syndrome caused by bacteria or viruses at a non-acute but high stress level. *Bacteria and viruses stay dormant if your immune system is functioning well.* Because the 'typical American lifestyle' drags you down, you cannot handle body invaders well. Lymes organism from deer ticks, mosquitoes and fleas is an example of an undiagnosed cause of fatigue, since the blood test is considered inaccurate both positive and negative.

- **Fatigue from sleep deprivation** from not getting uninterrupted 4 - 4 ½ hours of deep sleep before 4 AM. The health aspects of your bed make a huge difference in restful sleep. Wear ***ONLY*** natural fiber night clothing and use ***all natural bedding.*** A typical 'chemical' mattress is made primarily from crude oil and natural gas derivatives: polyurethane, Styrofoam, polyester, dyes, fire retardants and a host of other chemicals that makes restful sleep **A JOKE!!!** Call 1-800-Janices for organic *barrier cloth covers* for your mattress and pillows ... *and shower at night to reduce dead skin cells that feed dust mites that can wake you up!*

- **Taking supplements that are 'from chemicals' instead of 'herbs and whole food'** adds to chemical over load. *Poorly absorbed supplements require valuable body energy* *to be eliminated.* Find someone in your area with a SpectraVision biofeedback system, or other biofeedback system that can determine if the supplements you want to take are **compatible with your chemistry.** *You can also purchase books on Biokinesiology muscle testing to help you test (at home or in the health food store) the compatibility of products with your body.*

— **Retained toxicity due to lack of exercise is a leading cause of fatigue.** *The two things that move the lymphatic system are water and exercise.* Inflammatory symptoms are always an indication that you have a buildup of toxic wastes in your lymphatic system. *YOU CAN WALK OFF A COLD OR FLU!!!*

— **Dehydration is another leading cause of fatigue** from retained toxic wastes and poor digestion. *For inflammatory symptoms, add an extra glass to your daily requirement … and walk 30 minutes 3-4 times per day until you feel better!!!*

— **Low energy means fatigue,** so massage your Energy Healing points *1-3 x daily LIFETIME to calm your Triple Warmer and keep your energy up!!!*

ENERGY IS PRICELESS!!!

PUT BLAME FOR ENERGY LOSS WHERE IT BELONGS

I have a strong sense of spiritual direction to teach people how to help themselves and others in this national health crisis, affecting all Americans in some way. I believe our society desperately needs to **take a stand against** our shocking health statistics. ***WHY*** *is our country out of control on all levels of morals; spiritual connection (this is positively growing); mental, emotional and physical self-awareness.* You just have to listen to the news, or read a newspaper to hear about child and adult crisis situations **EVERYDAY!** You never hear about the outrageous obsession children and adults have with poor health choices **EXCEPT TO JOKE ABOUT THEM!** *It is sad that in this country someone who is interested in healthy choices is too often called a 'health nut.'* The typical American lifestyle choices result in an epidemic of diseases with people flocking to the medical profession for crisis control. **WE ARE A SOCIETY BLINDLY SEARCHING IN THE WRONG PLACES FOR ANSWERS TO INSANE SOCIAL BEHAVIOR.** We teach our children not to run into the street, and then feed them refined, chemical junk food that can only make them more unresponsive to other daily teachings. Relationships, careers and social pressures are often being handled by people who themselves have **EXHAUSTING** chronic health problems. Pacifying the self with social temptations is easy in a mentally and physically exhausted body. *Here is a list of issues* ***we*** *need to look at, that influence our energy on a cellular level:*

- **We need to look at** how hard work and goals are interrupted by disease because people have not learned to pace themselves living the 'American Dream.'

- **We need to look at** how often our *energy level* does not keep up with our hopes and dreams … **and we spend our lives wishing for what might have been.**

- **We need to look at** our intake of social drugs and addictive habits that influence both the individual and family members.

- **We need to look at** our intake of prescription drugs that are not given for acute life saving reasons. *ALWAYS INSIST ON WHY YOU HAVE A CHRONIC SYMPTOM AND BE UNWILLING JUST TO BLOCK THE SYMPTOM.*

– **We need to look at** the poor quality of many supplements that cannot help.

– **We need to look at** our exposure to electromagnetic polluted frequencies in our industrialized world that rob us of our energy.

– **We need to look at** the chemical overload we have created in the past 50 years in our food, water, clothing and environment.

– **We need to look at** the changes we have made with too many positive and too few negative ions from our 'new and improved' world and cement cities.

– **We need to look at** our children and ask ourselves why they are having adult diseases, and why a leading unit being added to hospitals across this country is cancer wards for children. **We need to look at** children who admire bullies and fanatics instead of spiritual leaders or health teachers.

– **We need to look at** kidney dialysis units being added to many hospitals to support kidneys that can no longer handle the insanity of modern America.

– **We need to look at** the decline in family unity.

There is no humor on this page … this is not funny!

ENERGY LOSS FROM SIMPLE MINERAL DEFICIENCIES

Politics and the big business of disease have led Americans down a challenging path. Not enough time and money is spent on teaching the **CAUSE** of any health crisis. **TOO OFTEN THE AMERICAN DREAM CAN BECOME THE AMERICAN NIGHTMARE.** We need to **wake up** and realize that what we are doing **IS NOT WORKING!** How many more adults and children will lose the quality of life … or die, before we learn some valuable lessons on the **PREVENTION OF DISEASE!** *Many health tips that are given to the general public are too few, too late for many, too incomplete and too fragmented to support the body as a whole, and be of lasting value.* We blame our frustrations on the wrong things because of our national standards and lost spiritual values. *No one seems to know how to stop the runaway train.* **Never before in the history of the world has there been a greater need for health recommendations that <u>simply work</u>!** *Health is simple … it is disease that is so complicated!*

One of my favorite research books has been **THE CHEMISTRY OF MAN** by Bernard Jensen., Ph.D. Dr. Jensen watched patients recover and thrive in over 50 years of work, when their diets were adjusted to provide the chemical elements their bodies needed. **HOW SIMPLE IS THAT!!!** Dr. Jenson's research showed some of the mental and emotional symptoms that can be caused by **simple mineral deficiencies:**

- CALCIUM (the 'knitter') – memory reduction, antisocial conduct, impatience, apprehension.
- CARBON (the 'builder') – unfeeling, bitter, unfriendly, overcritical, poor judgment.
- CHLORINE (the 'cleanser') – gloom, low self-esteem or spirit, everything out of balance.
- FLUORINE (the 'anti-resistant element') – awkward and vulgar but person convinced he/she is polished and graceful, false confidence.
- HYDROGEN (the 'moisturizer') – difficult to please, temperamental, intolerant.
- IODINE (the 'metabolizer') – tired, depressed, frustrated, imbalanced emotions.
- IRON (the 'frisky horse') – self-pity, antisocial, memory deficient, nervous stress, short temper.
- MAGNESIUM (the 'relaxer') – hyperactive, nervous personality, moods not grounded, life seems uninteresting.

- MANGANESE (the 'love element') – mental confusion, quarrelsomeness, impatience, unstable.
- NITROGEN (the 'restrainer') – hypochondriac with every ache exaggerated, mind is changeable, focus on extremes with nothing in the middle.
- OXYGEN (the 'giver of life') – nervous, emotional instability, stubborn, hypersensitivity, secretive, ill-tempered.
- PHOSPHORUS (the 'light bearer') – self-pity, morbidity, hypersensitivity, craves affection but self conscious.
- POTASSIUM (the 'great alkalizer') – fears, changeable moods, mostly negative, low drive.
- SILICON (the 'magnetic element') – depression, mental strain, brooding, hopeless, argumentative and ungratified.
- SULFUR (the 'heating element') – irritability, worry, stormy emotions, impulsive.
- SODIUM (the 'youth element') – mental confusion, mental exhaustion, quarrelsome, dull, disinterested, depressed.

These are often heard statements: "That's how he/she is." … or "What can I say, he/she is a teenager." … or "He/she always acts that way." … or "It's that time of the month."… or "He/she use to be so different, and I do not know what happened." … and the list goes on and on and on. **We too often make excuses for our own behavior … or others, without accepting responsibility for 'choices' that may have contributed to the mental or emotional state. Keeping up with social standards in America has become a poor health nightmare!!!**
    THE SOLUTION IS SIMPLE … PUT POSITIVE ENERGY INTO YOUR BODY INSTEAD OF DEPLETING YOUR BODY OF ENERGY:

- **DRINK THE CORRECT AMOUNT OF FILTERED AND ENERGIZED WATER DAILY.**
- **EVALUATE YOUR URINE AND SALIVA pH AT LEAST WEEKLY SO YOU HAVE SOME IDEA THAT WHAT YOU ARE DOING IS WORKING FOR YOU.**
- **KEEP THE ORGANS OF ELIMINATION LIKE THE LUNGS (DEEP BREATHING), BOWELS (DAILY ELIMINATION BEFORE NOON), KIDNEYS (DRINK YOUR CORRECT AMOUNT OF ENERGIZED WATER DAILY), AND LYMPHATIC SYSTEM MOVING DAILY (CHOOSE A WALKING TYPE EXERCISE 30 MINUTES EVERYDAY, OR USE A BALANCE BALL OR ROCKING CHAIR).**
- **KEEP THE SKIN CLEAN AND HEALTHY DAILY WITH A SHOWER OR BATH (GET A SHOWER OR BATH FILTER IF USING CITY WATER). USE NATURAL, ORGANIC SKIN CARE PRODUCTS.**
- **REDUCE CHEMICAL OVERLOAD BY EATING ORGANIC OR ALL NATURAL FOOD WHENEVER POSSIBLE!!! USE LESS CHEMICAL**

AND MORE NATURAL HOUSEHOLD PRODUCTS, AND WEAR MORE NATURAL FIBER CLOTHING.
- **GET ENOUGH REST ... 4-4 ½ HOURS OF UNINTERRUPTED SLEEP BEFORE 4 AM!!!**

If you think the above recommendations do not sound simple, consider the complications of having unnecessary stressful family issues that challenge or destroy the family unit ... or straining the family budget with challenging expenses ... or having a serious disease ... or ... losing the quality of life ... or life itself far too soon. There are many recommendations in this manual that assist in your wellness. All changes in your normal routine takes time and determination to become your new routine, and any effort you put in will produce rewards. If you are not happy with your present state of 'wellness' then do not keep doing what you have been doing because it is easy and familiar ... DO SOMETHING DIFFERENT ... AND MAKE A DIFFERENCE THAT YOU CAN LIVE WITH IN A WAY THAT MAKES LIFE JOYFUL!!!

FLOURIDATION CAN CAUSE ENERGY LOSS

This information is from an article by biochemist Dr. Yiamouylannis, Ph.D, who is recognized as an international authority on the biological effects of fluoride. He has served as Science Consultant on fluoridation in the US and abroad. Fluoridation is the addition of fluoride to the public water systems, at the rate of about 1 part fluoride for every million parts of water. Industries stuck with fluoride as a waste product originally promoted it as a means of reducing tooth decay. **Is that form of fluoride the answer?** Fluoride sources besides drinking water include treatments at the dentist, toothpaste, fluoride tablets or drops, mouthwashes, pesticides, Teflon-coated cookware, chewing tobacco, some wines, some sparkling mineral waters and tea (especially instant tea).

Chemical fluoride is more poisonous than lead, just slightly less poisonous than arsenic and right up there with mercury in poisonous effects in the body. A spokesman from Proctor and Gamble, the makers of Crest, acknowledges that a family-sized tube of fluoride toothpaste contains enough fluoride to kill a small child. While no one is going to die from drinking one glass of fluoridated water, just as no one will die from smoking one cigarette, *it is the long-term chronic effects of glass after glass of fluoridated water that takes its toll in human health.* In an Illinois court case, the judge ruled that fluoridation created a risk of serious health hazards. The Physicians Desk Reference points out that dental fluorosis (mottling) may result in hypersensitive individual. *The problem is we are not addressing why we are becoming more sensitive to many things.*

In 1992 the Canadian Dental Association's Proposed Guidelines did not recommend fluoride for children less than 3 years old. In 1990, 1991, and 1992, the Journal of the American Medical Association published 3 separate articles linking increased hip fracture rates to fluoridated areas. The March 1990 issue of the New England Journal of Medicine linked osteoporosis to fluoridated water. The ability of fluoride to transform normal cells into cancer cells has been confirmed by Argonne National Laboratories, which also found that fluoride increases the cancer-causing ability of other chemicals. Malfunctioning equipment does occur, as reported in 1979, when too much fluoride was pumped into the Annapolis, MD public water system poisoning 50,000 people. In 1993, the National Academy of Science admitted that up to 80% of the children living in fluoridated areas have dental fluorosis. A 1993 study by the US Public Health Service admitted the weight of the evidence leads to the conclusion that fluoride exposure results in genetic damage. A study published in the Journal of the American Chemical Society provided the chemical evidence to support that fluoride can damage biological chemicals like enzymes, leading to a wide range of diseases. During a court case in Scotland, both proponents and opponents of fluoridation confirmed that fluoride does weaken the immune system. Recent large-scale studies by public health dentists in New Zealand, Canada, and the US have reported tooth decay rates in fluoridated and nonfluoridated areas to be about the same. The October 1987 issue of the Journal of the Canadian Dental Association admitted that fluoridation isn't doing the job that dentists have been claiming it could do. In primitive societies, tooth decay is very low because of their low consumption of refined carbohydrates, like white flour and sugar. **It is quite evident that proper diet ... not fluoridation ... is necessary for good dental health.**

WHEN THE GERMS WIN YOU LOSE ENERGY

We are beginning to understand the serious limitations of the fight against germs. We are obsessed with killing germs at any cost to our present or future health. Bacteria mutate faster than science can make new killer drugs and products. Too often antibiotics are prescribed by 'guessing' there is a need; and we consume antibiotics in our food on a daily basis. This constant use of antibiotics has greatly affected the **terrain** of the intestine. On his deathbed, Pasteur said, *"The germ is nothing; the terrain is everything."* **Without healthy intestinal good bacteria, we can *think* we eat well and still be malnourished. We can take what we *think* are good supplements and still be sick.**

The stronger your overall body terrain is, the more resilient you are to disease. The typical American diet and use of chemicals has made our body terrain welcome hosts for viruses, bacteria, Candida Yeast, fungi and parasites, completing the process of decay that poor dietary choices and chemicals started. *We have set ourselves on a headlong collision course with germs …* **AND THE GERMS ARE WAY AHEAD!!!** They are winning because our use of germ warfare has upset the balance of nature. *In our germ killing frenzy we have created the new* **SUPER GERMS** *and at the same time we are weakening our body terrain.* Pesticides, herbicides, insecticides, lowered environmental oxygen, chemicals, chlorine and fluoride in our water and genetically engineered food are all examples of how we have messed up the world we were given. **WE MUST FIND OUR WAY BACK TO THE SIMPLISTICS OF HEALTH OR BE DESTROYED BY OUR TECHNOLOGICAL WORLD.** *This is not intended to replace needed medical attention, but consider the following as a place to start:*

1. **Stop** eating animal products containing hormone and antibiotics.

2. **Remember** the 'laws' of wellness, organic food, energized water and exercise.

3. **Take** supplements from natural sources and not made in some chemist lab.

4. **Take** a strong dairy-free probiotic product **every day** as discussed on page 37.

5. **Take** antibiotics only if tests confirm that the illness is <u>really</u> due to bacteria and not a virus, molds, allergic reactions or chemicals. *I've had seriously ill people in my office who **did not respond to antibiotics** and I was able to improve their health in less than one week with the following recommendations:*

- Walk 30 minutes 3-4 x a day so the lymphatic system cleans up the toxins.
- Use adrenal products I referred to on page 23
- Use thymus support that controls inflammatory symptoms by tapping the thymus gland for 15-30 seconds at the top of the breastbone every ½-1 hour. For a serious inflammatory disease consider ProBoost, a fabulous thymus booster product from Longevity Science (1-800-933-9440).
- Study Homeopathic remedies that raise your vital force (body energy).
- Increase the daily energized water amount by one glass until symptoms better.
- Encourage affirmations 4 x a day, "Everyday I am getting better and better."

When we forget what is natural to support optimum health, we begin supporting disease. In desperation, we turn to heroic measures that gamble with life itself. *Except in an acute crisis, we cannot eliminate threats to the body by force or we exhaust ourselves even more.*

ENERGIZE YOUR CIRCULATORY SYSTEM

This should be considered a top priority in your search for wellness. Common health concerns that send millions to the doctor for crisis control may be due to years of toxic build-up of heavy metals, pollutants or chemicals in your blood, arteries, heart, brain, kidneys, liver or other vital organs. *You are treated for the crisis rather than the cause of the symptom.* **My intent is not to diagnose, treat, cure or prevent any disease, but to provide information that <u>assists</u> in normal body function.** As a health-conscious person, chances are you already know cholesterol sludge is a big threat to your arteries and heart; about the dangers of mercury, lead and chemicals in your food and water plus a multitude of other unhealthy exposures you face every day. *YOU NEED TO LEARN HOW TO SURVIVE LIVING IN MODERN AMERICA AND PROMOTE NORMAL BODY FUNCTION SO YOU DO NOT DEVELOP A HEALTH CRISIS.*

CHELATION will soon be a household word. You may have been bombarded by mailings about oral chelation supplements that promise to 'clean out your arteries' and provide you with that elusive *fountain of youth formula. EDTA chelation works well intravenously and nutritionally monitored in a doctor's office.* Home use products of EDTA may strip you of valuable nutrients if you do not have correct hydration and digestion. I prefer **safer** formulas like a 100% natural **herbal** formula called *Cardio Vital Plus.* **If you are under medical care for any heart or circulatory condition, discuss using this product with your doctor.** You can get more information by calling 1-800-877-2434. Cardio Vital Plus should not be used if you are on blood thinners. **Remember circulatory health depends on exercise ... so never forget your 30 minutes daily ... or the other 'laws' of wellness!!!**

Thunder Ridge 100% Pure Emu Oil capsules is a natural choice for heart and vascular health; safe for people with seafood allergies. Emu Oil provides a complete source of essential fatty acids that must be obtained from the diet. Essential fatty acids contribute to heart and vascular health, and are vital to the energy you need for a healthy body. Other brands of essential fatty acids I recommend in my office are Krill Oil (shellfish) from Longevity Science (1-800-933-9440) and high concentrated Omega 3 fish oil products from Nordic Naturals (1-800-662-2544). If you have immune, heart, circulation or joint problems look for products highest in EPA; brain, eyes, and emotional symptoms look for highest DHA; skin, hair, hormone and metabolism symptoms look for highest GLA. *Taking the right product can make a lot of difference!*

A safe nutritional product that supports circulatory health is garlic taken daily. The brand I use in my office is Garlitrin 4000 that is available in most health food stores. I saw a TV interview of twins celebrating their 'over 100' birthdays and when asked to what they attribute their longevity, they said, *"We eat garlic every day."*

Find a local doctor with biofeedback testing equipment like the SpectraVision that helps choose nutrients **you need to balance your chemistry. DO NOT IMBALANCE AN ALREADY IMBALANCED BODY. SHOP SMART FOR NUTRITIONALS FROM KNOWLEDGE ... NOT GUESSING; LEARN BIOKINESIOLOGY MUSCLE TESTING FOR SUPPLEMENTS!**

ENERGY COMES FROM CORRECT CALCIUM BALANCE

Did you know that calcium was slowly turning you to stone? As we age, calcium is building up everywhere in the body ... called 'the aging process.' Anytime calcium builds up too fast out of solution due to low magnesium, you can get kidney stones, gallbladder stones, arthritis, sore muscles, memory loss and wrinkles in the skin. *The aging process is a normal process ... the trick is not to have it happen faster or sooner than you can manage.* A young child's muscles are soft and flexible because there is no calcium build-up yet. *As we get older, we develop 'knots' in our muscles that stay there and hurt!* Muscles become rigid and hard and a common comment among too many people in their 60's and 70's is, "*I'm not as limber as I used to be.*" **The ultimate example of this is rigor mortis when a person dies.** All the remaining calcium floods into the muscles and the body then becomes hard. *When a person is diagnosed with fibromyalgia they have painful, hard calcium knots in the muscles all over their body.*

Many people are calcium deficient because of dehydration, pH imbalance, poor dietary choices and stress that all result in poor digestion and absorption of nutrients. **Even with a calcium deficiency, calcium can be leached from your bones and teeth, and then deposited into your organs, muscles and arteries.** The average man or woman can lose up to 40% of their bone mass by the time they are 75 years old. **WHOA!!! By now all you want to know is what to do to prevent this process from causing you to speed up your aging process.** *Your 'fountain of youth' program may need some ideas, and here are some helpful suggestions:*

1. We've talked about DAILY exercise to move the lymphatic system, but *2-3 times a week you should include some **weight bearing exercises***.

2. Consider **oral chelation** products like the Cardio Vital Plus discussed on page 75. The loss of circulation is nearly identical to the signs of aging. By keeping the tiny capillaries open, the whole body can get what it needs to function (nutrition in and toxic wastes out) and reduce the signs of aging.

3. Consider **magnesium citrate powder** every night as discussed on page 25. Magnesium helps keep calcium in solution so it does not precipitate out and create stones, bunions, bone spurs and muscle knots.

4. **Be very careful not to consume too much calcium in multiple supplements.** We

have become a society obsessed with getting enough calcium. The result has made people drink allergenic milk with hormones and antibiotics and flock to the health food store for calcium containing products. Unfortunately many calcium products are poorly absorbed because they are look-a-likes made in a chemist lab and not derived from 'alive' foods. *Many calcium supplements are treated in the body like drugs and not physiologically supporting nutrients like food.* ***WE HAVE TECHNOLOGICALLY GONE BACKWARDS IN OUR PRODUCTION OF TOO MANY NUTRIENTS THAT ARE NOT COMPATIBLE WITH HUMAN CHEMISTRY BUT HAVE BEEN PRODUCED FOR PROFIT!!!*** *Read the Supplement Chapter in "The Power to Heal'* ... **FOLLOW THE 'LAWS' OF WELLNESS, THE ENERGY TIPS IN THIS MANUAL AND YOU WILL GET CALCIUM AND A WHOLE LOT MORE ... NATURALLY!!!** Dr. Dori Naturopathic Practitioner – 31

INCREASE YOUR ENERGY WITH STRESS MANAGEMENT

Stress is a killer. **We can't avoid being stressed, but we can control the damage from the stress response with four main minerals.** *Sodium and calcium turn on the stress response … and magnesium and potassium turn off the stress response.* **When these minerals are OUT OF BALANCE, stress gets out of control.** In 1840, a German scientist named Justus Von Liebig discovered that only nitrogen, potassium and phosphorus were put back into the soil, farmers could grow crops on the same piece of land over and over again without rotating crops. *Liebig is the father of artificial fertilizer that skyrocketed productivity and profit.* **The plants looked healthy because they could survive with just the three minerals and water, but people who ate those plants became mineral deficient.** If *WE* want to be healthy, we have to give the plants *ALL THE MINERALS* ***WE NEED, NOT JUST THE ONES THE PLANTS NEED.*** Commercial food is magnesium deficient. Without magnesium, you cannot turn off the stress response so people struggle with poor stress management. **ARE YOU NOW CONVINCED THAT YOU SHOULD EAT ORGANIC FOOD???**

Your nervous system has two main controls … one for normal stress days … and one for emergency stress situations. During a crisis, energy from any body system not involved in *immediate* survival is sacrificed, so energy can go where it is most needed to fight harder. *As far as the body is concerned, any acute **traumatic** situation, both emotional and physical, is treated the same as someone being mauled by a bear.* Modern day stress comes from polluted frequencies, chemicals, nutritionally deficient food, social and financial demands, acute and chronic ill health and trying to live 'the American dream.' *This can all cause poor digestion, a weak immune system, turns off the growth and repair systems, impairs sleep, obstructs circulatory function and hinders the production of hormones that help us deal with more stress.*

Cortisol is one of many hormones secreted by your adrenal glands in response to any type of stress. Its levels are normally highest in the morning to wake you up and lowest at night to let you sleep. If your levels are low in the morning you will have a hard time waking up and could feel tired all day. If your levels are high at night you could be depressed and have trouble sleeping. Your cortisol levels respond to daily stresses, but should re-adjust after each event. When your adrenals keep secreting this hormone inappropriately from constant stress or some medications, it can exhaust the adrenal glands … **and leave you feeling exhausted!!!** Besides that, excess cortisol pulls calcium out of your bones, puts you at risk for losing bone density and can be stored in abdominal tissue causing that middle bulge look. You can regulate cortisol levels naturally with the 'laws' of wellness and whole food supplements (not chemical look-a-like supplements that do not act in the body like food). The classification of supplement herbs called adaptogens plus the B Vitamins regulates your body's response to stress. Some herbs are nutritional, some are cleansing and some are adaptogens specific for stress management. Look for the word 'adaptogens' when shopping for herbal formulas to help you deal with the stressors of living in modern America. The Russians first discovered the value of adaptogen herbs that made them outstanding in space travel, Olympics and aging.

All higher brain functions become suppressed in stress, so you can concentrate on the 'fight or flight' emergency needs. We actually have three brains. The '**reptile brain**' is in charge of reflexes and survival and is 90-100% selfish. *Any negative emotion energizes the reptile brain.* When people are being controlled by that part of their brain, you cannot expect much cooperation out of them for your problems. The best thing you can do is just wait for things to pass, as moods always change. The '**mammal brain**' gives us emotions, social skills and is 50% or more cooperative, capable of some acts of self-sacrifice. *The mammal brain is the center for emotions, both positive and negative.* The '**human brain**' gives us language, reasoning and creativity. *We have large, powerful, creative, sensitive prefrontal lobes and we are capable of greater acts of love, creativity, unselfishness and cooperation than the rest of the creatures on this earth.* **Stress suppresses everything except the reptile brain, which beats the heart and moves the lungs.** You can not be as nice a person in a crisis (mammal brain suppressed), or as smart or creative (human brain suppressed)**. In a crisis you only need to survive.** This information, and a lot of other critical health awareness can be obtained from an excellent newsletter called The McAlvany Health Alert, April 2006. For subscription information call 1-800-464-1170 or go to www.mcalvanyhealthalert.com, and sign up for their free weekly email updates. The McAlvany Health Alert suggests these tips to help your bad moods pass quickly (functioning from the reptile brain) and help you discover your own genius and brilliance in your highest functioning mind (from the mammal or human brain):

1. Appreciation is a wonderful way to move the brain to higher functioning (out of the reptile brain).

2. Practice good moods. Appreciate the gift of life and enjoy the pleasures in your day (encourages the mammal brain). Even in a bad day you can thank God for the lessons to be learned.

3. Recognize when you are under stress … and actively cope with it. Focusing your attention on your feelings energizes your frontal lobes and you will react more intelligently.

4. Distract yourself by getting involved in something that interests you. When your mood lifts, ask your creative brain to come up with a useful and positive way of

dealing with a problem. Do not over think it!!! Ask the question and a good idea will come along.

All the energy producing information you learn will help you in some way to deal with the stress of social expectations in modern America and the stress from modern technology. **The one result I consistently get from my wellness program is my clients admitting that they are calmer and deal with stress better.** There is not one single recommendation, but **all the 'laws' of wellness** need to be understood in order to survive the challenges of recent decades. *Think of all the millions of people in America who do not understand what is happening to them.*

YOU ARE THE LUCKY ONE!!!

ENERGY LOSS FROM DUST MITES

The House Dust Mite is a relative of the spider and is found in all households even if the home is cleaned and dusted regularly. *Mites are microscopic and cannot be seen with the naked eye ... but they are there!!!* The biggest problem with dust mites is not the mite itself, but the fact that everyone is allergic to the mite's excrement. That means every time your body touches a mite's excrement, your adrenals have to make antibodies to protect you from the allergic reaction. ***WE NEED STRONG ADRENALS TO PROTECT US FROM 'MODERN AMERICA', SO ANYTHING YOU CAN DO TO TAKE THE STRESS OFF THE ADRENALS IS WORTH YOUR EFFORT!!!***

Mites can breed anywhere, but a favorite place is in the bedroom, in pillows, mattresses, duvets and blankets. ***Why do they love the bedroom?*** *Because in the bed they have a constant supply of dead skin cells for food and body moisture for their water from humans and animals.* Since we spend 8 hours a day in our beds, they have a great home ... and we have allergic reactions that can stress the immune system and interfere with our precious sleep. The tiny mite droppings (allergen) are made airborne by our slightest movement in bed. It is when the allergen is airborne that it can be harmful. **When the allergen is inhaled or comes into contact with our skin, symptoms of asthma, eczema or other allergic conditions and immune stress can be triggered.**

Dr. John Maunder stated in November 1992, that *"a pillow of six years old can have one tenth of its weight consisting of old human skin, mold, dead mites, living mites and mite dung."* My son worked as a Kirby vacuum salesman to make money while he was in college, and he did very well. He would ask a prospective buyer if he could vacuum their mattress and got such a pile of debris that he made many sales with ease. *A double bed mattress can have over 2 million Dust Mites living in the uppermost layers of the fabric*. ***SO WHAT IS A PERSON TO DO?***

Conventional sheets, pillow cases and duvet covers do **NOTHING** to protect you from the dust mite. The best way is to place an impermeable barrier between you and the problem. I suggest you call 1-800-JANICES and request a catalog, or you can just talk to them over the phone and tell them you want an organic barrier cloth cover for your mattress (state the size) and your pillows. You might find barrier cloth covers at local department stores, but they may not be organic and might contain chemical treatment of the material. For example, 100% Perma Press cotton sheets sound natural, but they are treated with formaldehyde to reduce wrinkling and that does not wash out.

The following helps reduce bedding mites:

— Vacuum your bed with your vacuum cleaning attachment monthly.
— Wash any mattress pads monthly.
— Wash your sheets and pillow cases weekly.
— Shower or bathe nightly to remove dead skin cells that feed mites. If you cannot shower or bathe, at least do a brisk rubdown with a towel and wipe skin off with a damp washcloth.
— Do not allow animals to sleep in your bed ... *sorry.*
— **ORDER YOUR BARRIER CLOTH COVER FOR YOUR MATTRESS AND PILLOWS TODAY!!!**

ENERGY LOSS FROM CHEMICALS …SURVIVING PESTICIDES

Not all references to being sensitive mean mental or emotional. **There are biological explanations for other kinds of sensitivities.** Some people with hyperactive nervous systems react stronger to chemicals than others. We **BELIEVE** we tolerate toxins in the air we breathe, the water we drink, the food we eat, the chemically based clothing we wear and the chemicals in the household products we use. *If you suddenly become sensitive to an exposure you thought was previously tolerated, it could be a warning sign that your digestive, elimination, circulatory and immune systems have been weakened for too long.* Every day you come in contact with toxins from chemical products that you've used for years and may not think to blame on your recent change of health. A build up of toxic chemicals can produce any chronic symptom that the doctors cannot trace back to a definite cause. *Rather than frantically trying the latest advertised 'detox' product,* **first reduce your exposure to the toxins in everyday products you use.**

Pesticides include insecticides, herbicides and fungicides. Farmers us 1.5 billion pounds of pesticides every year and most have been found by the *U.S. Environmental Protection Agency (EPA)* to be carcinogenic. The EPA has registered close to 900 pesticides, which are formulated into over 20,000 products according to the *Northwest Coalition for Alternatives to Pesticides.* One pesticide classification used in agriculture called organochlorines, acts like estrogen and has been linked to breast cancer. *The Lancet* December 1999 found a correlation between exposure to organochlorines and pancreatic cancer (on the rise for the first time in history). In her book, *Chemical Sensitivities,* Dr. Sherry Rogers explains that when pesticides **break down,** they produce substances called 'metabolites' that are *more toxic than the original toxins used to kill pests.* Studies by the *National Academy of Sciences* and the *Environmental Working Group* found that children exposed to carcinogenic pesticides are at a high risk of future cancer and other studies determined that pesticide use was associated with an increased risk of childhood cancers. That helps explain why children's cancer wards are being added to hospitals all across this country. **ORGANIC FOOD IS CRITICAL, BUT ALSO CONSIDER ALL THE HOUSEHOLD PRODUCTS YOU USE!!! STOP BUYING PRODUCTS THAT SAY 'DANGER', 'WARNING', OR 'CAUTION.'**

I purchase all natural household and personal care products; and stores that carry these products are constantly growing. I use pure vegetable Murphy Oil Soap, an original 90 year old natural cleaner for both wood and non-wood surfaces. We all want to kill ants, but by attacking **their** nervous system, you may be attacking your own. Without my knowledge a pest control man put a product in my bathroom and I lost control of my neck muscles, but struggled with a hoarse voice for months even after removing the product. I wrote a newspaper article about using sugar and yeast to kill ants instead of dangerous chemicals and they misquoted me saying, *"Dori hates white sugar and she says let the black ants eat it."* **We do not need bad journalism in this country, but we do need a major reality check on the connection between pesticides and disease.** You can check the internet for healthy options to killing pests. **The more we demand healthier products, the more they will be available. BE A HEALTHY CONSUMER AND LET THE STORES KNOW WHAT YOU WANT TO BUY!!!**

ENERGY LOSS FROM CONTAMINATED FOOD

We would not eat food if we thought it was toxic ... but it can be. Being aware of the reality of modern times should make a **little knowledge of how healthy food can become toxic food smart education.** E-coli and other bacteria are the 'bugs' that cause food poisoning. If you do get diarrhea from food poisoning (or any cause), refer on page 27. The Centers for Disease Control receive about 40,000 cases of food poisoning a year, 1000 of them are fatal. It is estimated the unreported cases could raise the number of illnesses into the millions. *You cannot escape these bacteria.* You can reduce your exposure and with a strong immune system fight them off without getting sick. Even though guidelines set by the Food Safety and Inspection Service for handling meat and poultry has increased, it may not be enough to protect you completely. ***Here are some 'smart tips' to help protect you from bacteria and viruses on food:***

- **Do not** fix food that will be eaten raw with hands that have not been thoroughly washed or cut the food on a counter that has not been thoroughly cleaned.

- **Do not** use plastic or wooden cutting boards that can harbor organisms. The only safe cutting board is tempered glass. There are many with designs that compliment your kitchen and can be left out as decoration. I have 3 tempered glass cutting boards with chicken designs that look very nice around the counter.

- **Clean up** animal products that leak their juices on the counter, with throw away paper towels, then wash the counter thoroughly with soap and more throw away towels.

- **Choose** the animal product that is on the bottom of the pile next to the cooling coils at the market. Do not buy any meat that does not appear fresh or is discolored.

- **Do not** buy animal products that are close to the expiration date, because not all bacteria are destroyed by cooking; refrigerate leftover food immediately after eating.

- **Think ahead** what meat you want the next day, and if frozen, let it thaw in the refrigerator overnight, rather than letting it sit out on the counter for hours.

- **Avoid** all raw animal products like oysters; raw sushi; raw dairy products; or raw eggs in appetizers, shakes, Caesar salads and Hollandaise sauce.

- **Do not** buy or use cracked eggs. Do not eat eggs that are not thoroughly cooked.

- **Do not** run errands after food shopping; take food home immediately.

- **Do not** serve animal products that are not cooked well … pink centers may not be healthy on beef, pork, buffalo, deer or lamb.

- **Wash your hands and kitchen utensils well** after handling animal products.

- **Never lightly wash** and then use the **same** kitchen utensils on raw vegetables **after** cutting meat.

- **Avoid** sponges that are a **breeding ground** for bacteria and viruses. I use a dishcloth rinsed in hot, soapy water after each use. After the dinner dishes are finished and the counters wiped off, the dishcloth and dishtowel goes onto a drying rack until laundered. **NEVER USE A DISHCLOTH OR DISHTOWEL MORE THAN ONE DAY BEFORE LAUNDERING.**

- **Take probiotics** discussed on page 37 that are *the ultimate defense against bacteria in food and your ability to maintain a strong immune system.*

With a little effort you can protect your energy in an imperfect world that is swarming with bacteria and viruses.

ENERGY FROM NATURAL FOOD SUPPLEMENTS

If you went to a health food store and looked at the rows of supplements ... OR read all the supplement advertising in your frequently stuffed mailbox ... OR talked to your friends who may not pass along accurate advice, you are thoroughly confused. Even worse, if you <u>supplement</u> shop at a grocery store, discount or chain store, you are most likely getting products that are incompatible with **YOUR CHEMISTRY ...** but very compatible with the supplement company and the store owner's profit. *Every company tries to convince you their products can pull off the 'fountain of youth' promise.* Even doctors' offices carry **<u>what you assume</u>** are good supplements because ... *a doctor recommended them.* **Unfortunately, commercial and profit seeking companies are interested in ... guess what ... profit!!!** In the Spring 2006 Health & Healing Consumer Alert newsletter by Julian Whitaker, M.D., it states, *"Is alternative medicine selling out? Natural healing has achieved so much and we've never needed it more. But is this lifesaving crusade turning into a cynical gold rush? Hordes of hucksters are swarming in, peddling unproven 'cures' that cost hundreds or thousands of dollars per month ..."* Robert Rowen M.D., in his Consumer's Heart Health News (available 1-800-728-2288) Winter Issue 2006 states, *"In independent lab test 57% of policosanol brands (for cholesterol) tested FAILED to meet basic standards. Some contained as little as 23% of the amount of policosanol listed on the label! It's bad enough these sleazy supplement makers are cutting costs by cheating on their potencies. But they're also using cheap substitutes to pump up their profits. And they're skimping on one crucial ingredient that's essential to getting the results you want."* Since biofeedback equipment to verify the compatibility of a product with **your** chemistry is not yet in most doctors' offices, they are **GUESSING ... BASED ON A SALES PITCH OR PRINTED ADVERTISING ... AND NOT ON YOU AS A BIOCHEMICAL INDIVIDUAL!!!** *So what supplement lines can you trust???*

I admit there are good natural food supplement lines that I do not carry in my office. However, I have found as a general rule, that as much as 80% of what people bring to their appointment does not test good for **THEIR CHEMISTRY** on my biofeedback machine. **Food is the primary factor in nutrient delivery and utilization.** *Most commercial supplements are made in a chemist lab and are look-a-likes to a fraction of a whole complex. In that form they are treated in the body like a drug and not as a physiologically supporting nutrient like supplements derived from food sources.* Because of the intense competition among so many supplement companies, *price has become the most important feature of their product line ...* **and lower prices mean lower quality!!!** Supplements derived from food sources cost more to manufacture, so commercial profit seekers have hopped on the 'money train' given the current health trends and are more interested in your purchase, than the value you receive. People trying to get well keep taking these *less expensive drug like supplements* in hopes of a miracle ... with too often disappointing results. *Read Supplement Guidance in my book 'The Power to Heal.'* You can also buy a book on Biokinesiology muscle testing and learn how to test your energy compatibility with the energy of the supplement. *If the supplement is good for you, your arm will be very strong ... and if the energy of the supplement weakens you, you will be weak on the arm testing.* I can recommend some companies that always test well on my biofeedback machine:

1. There are many nutritional quart juice products on the market that are raving about their health benefits. I have tested all of them in my office on biofeedback equipment and found most to be compatible with human chemistry but weaker than the same juice that is 100% pure. Noni, Goji, Acai, and Mangosteen are just a few examples that should be 100% pure juice and have no fruit juice sweeteners as additives. Because too many people are not digesting well, not exercising enough, not drinking enough healthy water and eating chemicals for food, the profit seeking health industry makes a big effort to sell expensive products that would not be necessary with healthy living choices on a daily basis. The cost of monthly supplements can get out of hand for one person or a family. I do not recommend you buy expensive supplements when you are not following the free 'laws' of wellness in this manual. One product I found that contains the above healthful juices and a lot more, plus reasonably priced is Reds Pak from Trace Minerals Research, 801-731-6051 or www.traceminerals.com. They also carry Greens Pak loaded with alive nutrients, is organic and vegetarian. Many health food stores now carry Reds Pak and Greens Pak.

2. *For over 30 years* **MEGAFOOD** *has been a leader in providing pure, bio-available and effective food nutrients. Megafood was the first company in 1973 to recognize the importance of natural food sources in the delivery of nutrients.* **Their supplements are organic, vegetarian, soy free, 100% whole food derived or herbal and highly absorbed.** They have a number of nutritional supplements that are generally safer for anyone who is not able to test on Biofeedback equipment. Medi-Safe is free of iodine, iron and safe for people on blood thinners. Herb Free Baby & Me is the best formula I've found for expectant or nursing mothers. Their whole foods B Complex or Un Stress always tests well and is a must product to help handle stress ... or if you are on birth control pills. The whole line tests excellent on my biofeedback system if the person needs that particular product. **Any company that goes to the expense of making it vegetarian will be more conscious of other quality control factors.** Check MegaFood out by calling 1-800-848-2542 or www.megafood.com. **This is a company I recommend without hesitation because they use full color spectrum food-based nutrition that is the next best thing to eating whole food, is organic, soy and dairy free, and is available is most health food stores or health pharmacies.**

3. **ROYAL BODY CARE** *is a multi-level company* that requires a distributor number to order. You can use mine (10984) because I am **not interested in building a business and you will never get called or pressured by me to buy more than you want … or be a distributor.** They sell Organic Spirulina that is extremely well absorbed if you have digestion problems. Spirulina is one of the few foods on earth you can live on with just it and water. *I consider Royal Body Care the highest quality source for Organic Spirulina and Spirulina based supplements.* They sell Spirulina power by the pound to put into blender drinks. The contact number for all their excellent products is 1-800-722-0444.

4. Two supplements worth considering are **SPROUTED FLAXSEED** that is better absorbed than any other version of flaxseed; and **MACA** capsules to balance all the glands and provide the adaptogen activity that protects you from stress. Both products are available in many health food stores.

5. **PURE ENCAPSULATIONS VITAMIN D3** may be an important supplement addition because we spend so little time outdoors year around and are obsessed with sun blockers. I read an article that states many babies are born with a Vitamin D deficiency because of not enough sun or too much sun blocker used by the mother. Make sure you are getting Vitamin D3 (cholecalciferol), and not D2 (ergocalciferol) found in synthetic vitamins. If you feel pain pressing firmly on your sternum (breastbone), you may be suffering from Vitamin D deficiency that may be the single most underrated nutrient involved in many health concerns like calcium absorption that controls pH. The dose during the winter months (or even year around if you are mostly an indoor person) is minimum 4000 mg. daily. PURE ENCAPSULATIONS sells hypo-allergenic supplements and is a company to look for when you do not know how to trust supplement companies. They make a hydrochloric acid and pepsin product that is hard to find vegetarian; and pure MSM powder that helps the whole digestive system and any inflammatory condition. Many health food stores carry Pure Encapsulations products.

6. **LONGEVITY SCIENCE** is a therapeutic supplement line I use in my practice. You may contact them at 1-800-933-9440 if direct mail works for you. Their Magna-Calm works wonders for constipation. They also sell therapeutic grade products like Enteropro that is a highly absorbed probiotic and essential fatty acid product called Krill oil. Their Q10 product Advanced Q10 is only one of two Q10 products that test best on my biofeedback system for absorbability … the other one is from Vitaline. Carnitine is a supplement that supports intracellular energy but is usually found in a beef capsule. Longevity Science has formulated Carnitine in vegetarian capsules.

7. Many commercial supplements have animal sources of gelatin, glycerin, magnesium stearate or stearic acid from beef sources that stress your immune system … and make

your adrenals make antibodies every time you take the supplement. This continuous production of antibodies can set you up for an autoimmune disease anywhere in the body; check the following companies for their *vegetarian products* – **SOLGAR, NEW CHAPTER, PURE ENCAPSULATIONS, AND MEGAFOOD**.

8. **HOMEOPATHIC REMEDIES** are discussed on page 93. *A homeopathic is a process of dilution and one brand is not better than another… so homeopathic remedies in a health food store may be better choices than some herbs or supplements.* Supplements may not be compatible to your chemistry. Herbs could be processed so weak they pass the legal labeling requirements, but may be comparable to putting a house fire out with a squirt gun. This country started out with Homeopathic medicine. Then politics, traditional medicine and the race for wealth took over. *Now we are coming full circle back to Homeopathy.*

THE ENERGY OF HOMEOPATHY

IF YOU HAVE A SYMPTOM, YOUR VITAL FORCE IS DOWN! IT IS YOUR DEPRESSED VITAL FORCE, NOT YOUR SYMPTOM THAT IS THE ORIGIN OF DISEASE. Homeopathy is a method of stimulating the body's own healing process in order to allow the body to heal itself. The word "homeopathy" is taken from the Greek "homeos" meaning similar and "pathos" meaning suffering. Thus, homeopathy means to treat with something that produces an effect similar to suffering. *IT IS 'THE LAW OF SIMILARS' OR 'LIKE CURES LIKE.'*

Homeopathy holds that every person has a <u>vital or dynamic force,</u> which normally keeps the person healthy by maintaining a *normal balance of all systems* in the body, mind and spirit. Homeopathy thus defines **all disease** whether physical, mental or emotional, acute or chronic … **as derangements of the vital force in an attempt to restore balance.** This derangement occurs at such a subtle level that it cannot be directly perceived except through **'symptoms.'** *All symptoms are created by the vital force in its struggle to maintain balance and health.* **Homeopathic medicine views all symptoms, however painful or disagreeable as beneficial, in that they point out the *path* that the vital force has taken in its attempt to restore health.**

Homeopathy works on the principle of RESONANCE … like a singer who shatters glass on a special note that **MATCHES** the energy of the glass. The source of the homeopathic remedy can be any substance that has <u>proven</u> to have certain symptoms when taken in excess. When these symptoms **MATCH EXACTLY** the symptoms of the person, the **TWO** energies **combined** will increase the overall energy (called resonance). **This increased energy raises your vital force and you are now stronger to overcome the symptoms.** *The importance in homeopathy is to match ALIKE SYMPTOMS ON ALL LEVELS OF PHYSICAL, EMOTIONAL AND MENTAL.* The closer the match, the stronger the resonance. You will have no effect from the wrong remedy because there will be no resonance (like a singer who does not break glass). **To change the LEVEL OF HEALTH, change the person's constitution or VITAL FORCE** … *a subtle governing energy that organizes and directs physical and chemical action of the body.* The efficiency of a person's vital force is reflected in degrees of health or illness. *Visualize your vital force between two poles … the lower, as <u>sick</u> as you can get based on your current total health and hereditary factors … and the higher, as <u>healthy</u> as you can get based on your total health and hereditary factors.*

REMEMBER… SYMPTOMS ARE AN EXPRESSION OF YOUR VITAL

FORCE'S EFFORT TO HEAL. DO NOT SUPPRESS YOUR BODY'S ATTEMPT TO COMMUNICATE WITH YOU ... TUNE INTO BODY LANGUAGE!!! Drugs that suppress symptoms should be avoided if possible and only used in acute situations. *Just treating symptoms is masking the fact that your vital force is down; and you need to be dealing with **that fact**, rather than just temporarily wanting to feel better.* In an acute crisis the traditional approach is comforting and can be life saving. After the crisis we must always look for the **cause** of the body not working at optimum performance and how to assist the body in healing itself. *Turn the page to get started with your <u>Home First Aid</u> products using Homeopathy.*

HOMEOPATHIC SOURCES FOR VITAL ENERGY

You can now collect fast and effective Homeopathic remedies that will be your <u>First Aid Kit</u>, ready to be **your 1ˢᵗ line of defense.** In many acute situations, homeopathy may raise your <u>Vital Force</u> to encourage a healing process faster than anything else. There are *tips and tricks* to using these remedies and I suggest you invest in some *beginning Homeopathic books.* **This approach to ill health is not intended to treat or replace appropriate health professionals or medical advice.** *Homeopathy can often keep a simple symptom from becoming a crisis that requires more professional attention.* In Homeopathy it is the symptom that guides the remedy choice … while knowing the name of the disease is not necessary. *Homeopathy can be used for almost any symptom. Although serious illnesses should also be monitored by your health care professional, Homeopathy can be a fantastic compliment to your other treatment.* **You may find these sources helpful in your Homeopathic educational process:**

- **Homeopathic Healing Miracles** is a monthly publication that is a perfect place to start understanding Homeopathy, how to care for Homeopathic remedies and important remedies to have on hand for common emergencies. To order an annual subscription call 1-905-760-9929 ext. 300.

- **Washington Homeopathic Products** for a catalog and purchasing remedies. Call 1-800-336-1695 or www.homeopathyworks.com.

- **Standard Homeopathic Co.** for a catalog and products, 1-800-624-9659 or www. hylands.com. .

- **Homeopathic Educational Services for a catalog, books courses, tapes, software, and charts (an excellent one-stop source)** 1-800-359-9051 or www.homeopathic. com.

- **Find a local Homeopathic healer** who is certified, knowledgeable, patient and caring. Your health is important and your Homeopath holds your health in his/her hands … so make sure you find the most qualified. These sources may help you find the best in your area:

* **American Board of Homeotherapeutics** (US), charges for the list by calling 1- 703-548-7790 or it is free on www.homeopathic.org.

* **HANP** (US and Canada), 1-253-630-3338 or www.hanp.net/directory.html. You can also get some great resources in the links section www.hanp.net/links. html.

* **Health food stores** often carry Homeopathic 'formulas' that provide a number of remedy options specific for a particular problem like a cold, allergy, insomnia, injury, stress, etc. These formulas have multiple potencies, so your body can pick the one right for you. Formulas may work better for the novice unsure of the skill to pick a single remedy.

* The owner or manager of a health food store may know about **local Homeopathy groups, Naturopathic Doctors, or holistic Medical Doctors in the area.**

* **Pharmacies that carry Homeopathic medicines** may know local practitioners.

* **Alternative magazines and newspapers** are often available at health food stores; check the Yellow Pages. You are very lucky if you find a Medical Doctor or Naturopathic Doctor who practices Homeopathy! *Raising your vital force is the best way to produce the health improvement you seek.*

THE ENERGY OF BACH FLOWER REMEDIES

The body functions using energy on **all levels** of mental, emotional and physical. The Bach Flower Remedies are in the same category as other subtle methods of healing such as Homeopathy or herbal medicine. Edward Bach was a highly successful bacteriologist and Homeopathic physician. He gave up his lucrative medical practice in 1930 to search for a simpler, more natural method of treatment that did not require *anything* to be destroyed or altered.

Every physical, emotional or mental symptom gives us a particular message ... and we need to acknowledge these messages. **EVERY TRUE HEALING PROCESS IS AN AFFIRMATION OF OUR WHOLENESS.** The Bach Flower remedy system heals by restoring harmony in **AWARENESS.** When vital energies are channeled the wrong way or blocked with negative thoughts, the Bach Flower Remedies re-establish positive contact with our wholeness.

Bach Flower Remedies are different from other subtle methods of treatment in 3 ways:

1. They act more on the energy system rather than the physical body, dealing with ***disharmony in the soul*** in a more comprehensive way than Homeopathic remedies for mental and emotional symptoms.

2. The healing energies are released from the flowers in a way that there can be no overdose, no side-effects and no incompatibility with other methods of treatment. The plant itself is not destroyed or damaged. The flower containing all the essential energies of the plant is picked at full perfection when it is about to drop.

3. To use the Bach Flower Remedies calls for no training in medicine or psychology, but only the *ability to think and possess sensitivity and feeling.*

In 1943 Bach wrote the following incredible insight about his Flower Remedies:

"The action of these remedies is to raise our vibrations and open up our channels for the reception of the Spiritual Self; to flood our natures with the particular virtue we need, and wash out from us the fault that is causing the harm. They are able, like beautiful music or any glorious uplifting thing which gives us inspiration, to raise our very natures, and bring us nearer to our souls and by that very act to bring us peace

and relieve our sufferings. They cure, not by attacking the disease, but by flooding our bodies with the beautiful vibrations of our Higher Nature, in the presence of which, disease melts away as snow in the sunshine. There is not true healing unless there is a change in outlook, peace of mind, and inner happiness. Let not the simplicity of this method deter you from its use, for you will find the further your researches advance the greater you will realize the simplicity of all Creation. They who will obtain the greatest benefit from this God-sent Gift will be those who keep it pure as it is; free from science, free from theories, for everything in Nature is simple."

Bach felt that the true causes of disease are the 'defects' from our negative side such as pride, cruelty, hatred, self-absorbed, ignorance, greed, fear, jealousy, anger and worry. He said that two basic errors are the cause of disease:

1. Where the personality turns away from love, positive character traits are distorted and become destructive, leading to negative moods.
2. The personality turns against the 'principle of unity' and renders the sufferer a slave to his own body.

IF THIS DOES NOT SOUND PROBABLE, THEN UNDERSTAND AND ACCEPT THAT BACH FLOWER REMEDIES HEAL IN A WAY THAT <u>FIRST DOES NO HARM</u>. *Simplicity tends to be misunderstood in a world of increasing sophistication.* Simplicity has to do with unity, perfection and harmony. That is the reason everybody feels attracted to the *'simple things in life.'* The specific flower energy has the same wavelength as the energy of the Higher Self (*your subconscious mind*) wanting to express itself. The remedies are able to make contact with this part of your mind, washing over the current blockage at a lower **disharmonious** level and flooding it with its own higher **harmonious** frequency. This new reinforcement is now able to see things in a different light. **This is critical, since disharmony from negative mental and emotional thoughts is the beginning of disease.**

The test to determine what Bach Flower Remedy to consider is in the Positive Thinking chapter of my book 'The Power to Heal.' Bach Flower Remedies are sold in health food stores and can be ordered from the homeopathic sources listed on 38. **BACH FLOWER REMEDIES HELP YOU FIND YOUR TRIPLE P'S ...**

POSITIVE PERSONAL POWER!!!

The three things that control digestion are <u>positive thinking, water, and pH balance.</u> DIGESTION CONTROLS YOUR HEALTH!!! NEVER FORGET THAT IN <u>ANY</u> DISEASE THERE ARE ONLY TWO BASIC PROBLEMS:

– **NUTRITIONAL STARVATION**
– **TOXIC OVERLOAD**

**** YOUR THOUGHTS CONTROL BOTH OF THEM!

THE ENERGY OF COLOR

The need for recognition is plainly seen by the way we dress. Some people make a statement of individuality, others of success, others of sexuality and others of innocence. **OUR SELECTION OF COLORS IN ALL AREAS OF OUR LIFE DETERMINES OUR ACCEPTANCE OR REJECTION OF OURSELVES!**

"Color" refers to a mental and emotional interpretation of what the eyes see. Since sunlight sustains life and there is death without it, man has believed in the healing power of color since the beginning of recorded time. Color was associated with disease because disease produced color – red, inflammation; blue, cold; pale to white for illness; black, blue, yellow, green for degrees of injury. Light and color are being worked back into modern medicine such as infrared radiation for certain aches and pains, ultraviolet light for depression, and blue light to treat newborn jaundice.

Color is the **ESSENCE** of life force **ALL AROUND US!** The scientific use of color in our bodies introduces a natural ENERGY that promotes the elimination of waste products that helps repair cellular damage and encourages positive thinking and enthusiasm. *White is a combination of colors associated with pure, clean and cool. Black is the absence of color associated with neutrality and emptiness.* It is interesting that black has become the basic color in our stressful world. **Health is best achieved using the many shades of visible color that have a powerful influence on our health.** The two extremes of the color spectrum are:

- **RED** raises vital signs and excites body responses. **The hot or advancing colors are red, orange and yellow.**
- **BLUE** lowers vital signs and relaxes body responses. **The cold or receding colors are turquoise, blue and purple.**
- **GREEN is a neutral color.**

The following are ways color influences us:

- **THE FOOD WE EAT** - People who like very few brightly colored vegetables, and eat mostly meat, dairy, grains and starches are missing an important energy factor that promotes a healthy mind and body. Look at a plate of sliced meat, potatoes and gravy ... then add a spread of ripe red tomatoes and notice the difference in your interest. Stir-fry some rice and left over chicken ... then notice the difference when you add tomatoes, green and yellow squash, red or green peppers to the stir-fry. *Vitamins were discovered by the color present in them.*

– **THE COLORS IN OUR ENVIRONMENT** – If a person's surroundings are bright, that energy will be carried into daily living decisions. Warm colors are best in the kitchen, dining room, recreation and work areas. Cool colors are relaxing and best in the bedroom, sitting room, library or den. Finding a place of peace and quiet by the blue sea, or in a green forest will create more 'spring fever' than blazing creativity. **Colors do send signals.** *Have you ever seen a blue stop sign, a turquoise danger sign, or a green hazardous area sign?*

– **THE COLORS WE WEAR** – It helps to know what colors look best on your skin tone because you feel better when you look good. Find out if your skin tone is a Spring, Summer, Fall or Winter by being professionally color draped or reading a book on personal colors. It will save you money because you will not buy clothes on impulse, that once you get them home you do not understand why you do not enjoy wearing the item. **The way you dress is a 'color energy' expression of who you are!!!**

> *I worked in a psychiatric hospital in a teenage department and one day a young girl's family visited. They wanted to go out and buy her some clothes and she gave them detailed instructions of what she wanted. They returned with a pair of black jeans, black socks, a black top and black sweatshirt. She took the clothes to her room with no change in her expression.*

People are born to win…but they must first develop a good self image. Have more to look at when you open your closet than … is it clean, or is it pressed? **BE DYNAMIC … DRESS TO WIN AND TURN YOURSELF ON!!!**

RENEW ENERGY WITH PROPER GRIEVING PROCESS

The grieving process is a process of growing. Keep in mind that we grieve about many things besides the death of a loved one. We grieve about loss of a relationship, separation, divorce, loss of income or job, loss of goals, moving, retirement, aging, loss of health or youth, loss of beauty or hair, loss from a robbery or fire, loss of control in a situation, loss of hope or pride or self-worth. You can have potential losses like a person missing. *Under the burden of each sorrow we either grow … or we die a little each time.* The suffering can give us new strength … or it drains us and robs us of life. The Irish have a saying **"THE SAME FIRE THAT MELTS THE WAX HARDENS THE STEEL."**

Regardless of the reason for the grief, what happens is the most profound pain we'll ever experience. It can strike suddenly and cause havoc for months, years or a lifetime. It can stress our immune system and leave us vulnerable to disease. It can cause virtually every illness from acne to arthritis, headache to heart disease, cold sores to cancer. **ALL BODY SYMPTOMS ARE INFLUENCED FOR BETTER OR WORSE BY OUR EMOTIONS.**

Loss is part of our lives from our beginning when we suffer the loss of protection in our mother's womb … or weaning from breast feeding … or starting school and leaving a familiar routine. Some grieving is easier because it is final and opens up new experiences that help us grow, as time allows healing to occur. Some grieving is bearing a lifetime of unending suffering. *You can get stuck in any one of the first four stages of grieving …Denial … Anger … Bargaining … Depression … and never proceed to … Acceptance … that allows you to go on with your life.* Richard Bach, Author of "ILLUSIONS" said, **"THERE IS NO SUCH THING AS A PROBLEM WITHOUT A GIFT FOR YOU IN HAND."**

Some people are **natural survivors** and come through horrible challenges, becoming somehow enriched and renewed. *They all have things in common like choosing not to be a victim; using life's lessons as ways to become stronger; more into 'we' than 'I'; and concentrating on their contribution to mankind.*

The **'casualties'** who physically and emotionally collapse also have things in common. *They hold on to anguish and despair because 'they can't be happy, and life is hard;' they live in the past and have little energy for the present or future; they build memorials to their losses that gives them excuses for their behavior; they create a negative subconscious that traps them.* **Are you still grieving about something?** *There is this story example:*

Two celibate monks walking near a stream came across a young woman wanting to cross it. One of the monks, to the dismay of the other, picked up the woman and carried her across the stream. About a mile later, the monk who was aghast at the other's action asked how he could pick up a woman when they were supposed to be celibate. The monk replied that he had put the woman down a mile back; why was the other still carrying her around?

In any loss be gentle with yourself. You have had an emotional wound … but wounds heal if taken care of. **There are 3 primary needs for appropriate grief work:**

- **HAVE A COMMITMENT TO HEAL** – You cannot go forward by going backwards.

- **ACKNOWLEDGE YOUR SPIRITUAL THERMOSTAT THAT BALANCES EMOTIONS** – You can call your powerful emotional strength anything you want … but it is there when you need it.

- **UNDERSTAND THAT ENERGY IS OUR INWARD NATURE** – Find a way to experience again that feeling of 'getting it all together' that most people have enjoyed at some time during their life. *The redirection of positive energy is the first step through the grief process.*

The grieving person is mentally weary. An exhausted mind distorts reality and makes it easier to think negative thoughts because there isn't any energy left. *Our physical bodies, emotions and mind are intimately interacting. To ignore the needs of one will sabotage them all … in time.* When emotional pain hurts, you need to take very good care of yourself and make healthy choices for your well-being. A nutritionally deficient system becomes too sensitive and you react emotionally rather than think a situation through. **GRIEVING IS NOT TIME FOR JUNK FOOD!!!** *Caffeine and alcohol increase urination and deplete needed nutrients. Sodas rob you of calcium at a time when you need three times more calcium than when you are not in stress. This is a time when exercise is critical to get rid of the toxins produced by stress. This is a time to eat organic food, and not add chemicals to the burden your system is already experiencing.*

I used to teach a grieving class, and some of my material came from a class I took on grief management. The instructor's story is an example of growing through expressive grief work, having survived her husband's suicide and 4 years later her talented son's suicide. She says beautifully,

"We have our bodies with all our marvelous sensory gifts – movement, sound, and vision. We have our intelligence to make plans, study and seek outside help. We have our emotions – everything from apathy, desolation, alienation, to excitement, discovery and intimacy to use. We are equipped to live, learn and mature. If we

choose to break loose our stagnant energy, to become active rather than passive, to hope rather than abuse fate, then, by measure, we have passed one of the critical tests fulfilling our potential. The choice is mine … and yours."

IF YOU ALLOW YOURSELF TO BECOME STRONGER FROM THE LOSS OR EXPERIENCE, THEN IT GIVES SOME REASON AND VALUE TO THE PAIN YOU ARE FEELING. IT HELPS TO ANSWER THE QUESTION …WHY? IT GIVES PURPOSE TO THAT PART OF LIFE WE DO NOT UNDERSTAND. IT HELPS RENEW YOUR ENERGY!

ENERGY IS THE FOUNTAIN OF YOUTH

Correct nutrition produces energy ... and that is the fountain of youth. Americans often believe that a single drug, or technological procedure, or a trip to the vitamin shop can cure a disease or heal the body ... *and they blame hereditary weaknesses for everything.* However, all organs increase their level of activity in an attempt to compensate for the lowered activity of the weakest ones. For example, if you do not exercise ... the liver, kidneys, and skin work harder. In doing so, they all use more of the nutrients available and the whole body tends to become depleted.

Each organ obtains the nutrients it needs from the bloodstream ... **if** the nutrients are there based on the quality of what was eaten ... and digested ... and assimilated (food changed into a form the body can use). **IT ALL STARTS WITH WHAT YOU CHOOSE TO PUT INTO YOUR MOUTH!!!** You cannot digest and assimilate healthy nutrients if the nutrients were not <u>*first*</u> in the food you ate. Processed, chemically loaded and refined food fills the stomach ... but our health statistics suggest not enough nutrients get to the cells. *New and improved* only refers to the bank accounts of the food producers and distributors ... **you cannot improve on Nature.** *The typical American diet has become disease producing. On a recent trip, my husband and I stopped for gas early in the morning, and a man came out of the store with an extra large container of a soda drink and a bag of potato chips. Another morning we were walking to church and a man come out of a restaurant with a cup of coffee in one hand and an ice cream bar in the other.* **JUST BECAUSE YOU ARE NOT HUNGRY DOES NOT MEAN YOU HAVE CELLULAR HEALTH. WHEN YOU EAT ... THE FOOD MUST HAVE VALUE FOR YOU TO FEED THE CELLS!!!**

It is time we stop and think that the majority of the world population dies prematurely from diseases that develop due to nutritional deficiencies in the diet. That puts a whole new perspective on the subject of nutrition ... and for most Americans struggling with fatigue and disease it should be called 'newtrition.' *There is no substitute for proper nutrition and no therapy or healing art that can keep a malnourished body free of disease.* Do not waste an opportunity to '*feed your cells.*' First, buy organic so the food actually has the nutrients you expect in the food. The average housewife peels her vegetables, throwing away nutrients; then the food may be boiled and drained of even more nutrients, or 'nuked' in the microwave. **Treat your organic fruits and vegetables with respect for their life giving properties. Know that you are hydrated with energized water and your pH is in the normal range!**

We are what we eat … and we also are what we do not eat. The body molds to the foods we put into it … for better or for worse. Poor food habits that result in nutrient deficiencies in the brain could produce mild to bizarre misbehavior … or something as simple as low motivation that does not bring out your best strengths. *Poor nutrition is often at the root of undeveloped or underdeveloped talents.* The right foods, the right experiences and teachings awaken the brain centers and allows each human being to develop his or her full potential on this planet. ***YOU ARE SO LUCKY TO HAVE ALL THE BASIC KNOWLEDGE THAT CAN CHANGE THE ENERGETIC QUALITY OF YOUR LIFE … ENJOY IT!!!***

A STRONG IMMUNE SYSTEM SUPPORTS ENERGY

Most people will not escape getting the flu one or more times during their lifetime. There is a 'flu season,' but it can strike anyone, anytime during the year. For most people it is a relatively short period of misery. For others it can be incredibly serious requiring hospitalization … even death as the outcome. Your body comes with a 'flu shield' called the *IMMUNE SYSTEM*. **THE TRICK TO TREATING THE FLU IS TO PREVENT IT!!!** If your body is healthy, it can survive an outbreak in your home, your work or your community.

Knowing how your immune system works helps you better understand how to boost it with an organic diet, herbs, natural based supplements and Homeopathy. **Your immune system is your body's defense program designed to disrupt foreign agents that come into your body.** Your immune system recognizes the threat of invading bacteria and viruses that are looking for a place to breed … *and because this would be at the expense of body balance, your immune system eliminates or neutralizes the culprit.*

Since it is not easy to permeate the body's natural defense in the first place, your immune system knows the foreign agent is strong enough to break through the antibacterial and antiviral properties in the sinus, throat, and nasal mucous membranes. Mucous, tears, saliva and other body fluids wash away most microorganisms. If it gets past those, a fever offers an unsuitable environment for the organism to live. **NEVER SUPPRESS A HARD WORKING FEVER UNLESS IT IS LIFE THREATENING!** If you want to take something for a fever take the cell salt Ferrum Phosphoricum available in most health food stores. Ferr. Phos. carries oxygen that kills bacteria and viruses, and naturally helps your body handle the invasion. The acid condition in the stomach can also kill organisms that get past the mucous membranes.

The main line of defense in your immune system is the cells that fight infection. They rush to the infected spot, engulf the intruding organism and destroy it by consuming and digesting it:

1. **B CELLS** – Growing out of your bone marrow, B Cells produce protein antibodies that stop the foreign agents dead in their tracks.

2. **T CELLS** – Grow in your thymus gland and are primarily responsible for making cells immune to viruses. They secrete certain molecules that attract other immune cells to come to the place of infection and the *T Cells act as managers for all the defensive activity.* T Cells are always circulating … always on the look out for anything out of the ordinary.

3. **KILLER T CELLS** – They have a one track mind … to wipe out the foreign invader. They bind to the foreign invader and release enzymes that kill it. It is the Killer T Cells that have to be inactivated in organ transplants.

4. **HELPER T CELLS** – They act as switch operators, flipping the switch so the immune response starts moving and set the B Cells in motion. A great percentage of T Cells are Helper T Cells and are the ones targeted by HIV, making the body vulnerable to infection.

5. **SUPPRESSOR T CELLS** – These cells make sure the body does not get carried away with all the activity and regulates the immune response by adjusting or varying the intensity as needed.

6. **NATURAL KILLER CELLS** – They are your body's greatest weapon against infection and disease. They have free range throughout the body, with the ability to recognize and kill any foreign invader upon contact.

Your entire immune system is a series of checks and balances, with every defensive measure needing to be triggered by something and then backed up by another defense. **TRY RUNNING THAT COMPLICATED SYSTEM WITH A DONUT AND COFFEE FOR BREAKFAST!!!**

The incredibly important immune cells are the **front lines** of the immune response. In the **back lines** the organs that collectively make up the 'lymph system' include the bone marrow, thymus, spleen, tonsils and lymph nodes that are sprinkled throughout the body. *When you have an infection, the closest lymph node will swell up to contain the toxins.*

The immune system functions on its own without your conscious help. However, it needs to be kept healthy like your heart, bones or any other organ or system in your body. **The stress to the immune system is monumentally greater than it was even 50 years ago.** *Today … living in modern America … we need to make better choices to take some stress off the immune system, so it is there when we need it. Eating* **organic food** *and drinking* **filtered, energized water** *is a no-brainer in modern America.* **Daily exercise** *improves circulation allowing the T and B Cells to arrive on the scene of an infection quickly and put it down before it begins to multiply and cause you symptoms.*

STAYING ENERGETIC IS EASY IF YOU UNDERSTAND THE 'LAWS' OF WELLNESS!!! Why do people have to be ill or dying to start taking care of themselves? You earn your health and longevity by the choices you make … disease that you develop in your lifetime is not bad luck!!! Now look at your body and say, "Thank you immune system for all your hard work … and I'll take better care of you now." Little things collectively make a big difference like showering at night so your bed is not full of dust mites that produce allergic responses and make your adrenals work all night instead of resting. And, do not forget to thump your thymus gland on your breastbone 3-4 times a day. _**Be good to your body and your body will protect you!!!**_

AN AUTOIMMUNE DISEASE ROBS YOU OF ENERGY

Most people today have heard of the term '**autoimmune disease.**' I've had three medical doctors in my office say about 60% of the patients they see in their office have an autoimmune disease. *What is it and why it is becoming so common in modern America?* On page 107 you learned how strong the immune system is against foreign invaders. Imagine what could happen if the immune system started attacking its own body's cells. In an autoimmune disease the immune system mistakenly attacks its own body and targets cells, tissues and organs that are not foreign at all. **This happens when the overworked immune system works so hard to deal with your needs, that it makes '*mistakes.*'**

I am constantly reading articles that we have much to learn about autoimmune disease ... scientists are trying to find therapies that work on the body's immune response ... ultimately science hopes to find ways to prevent autoimmune diseases. I also read articles 20 years ago that said we could stop cancer. The reality of politics is that research and 'the ultimate cure' is more of a focus then the **simple rules of health** that encourage body **balance,** rather than having to deal with the complicated results of **imbalance.**

I suggest you look closely at the following suggestions that encourage your body not to need to make antibodies or deal with the prolonged stress of needing to make antibodies daily:

1. *Reduce* dust mites in your bed with a barrier cloth cover for your mattress and pillow, no animals in the bed, clean bedding weekly and shower nightly.

2. *Drink* your healthy energized water daily, instead of juices that may contain mold requiring your adrenals to make antibodies. Juice and coffee have become America's water ... and that can lead to disease.

3. *Eliminate* dairy products and beef which I have found to be allergic on everyone I've tested on my biofeedback machine for 18 years. America's obsession with dairy and beef often requires the production of daily antibodies.

4. *Eliminate* any other protein based food to which you have a known allergic reaction. If you suspect a reaction to a food you are eating, do the allergic test for foods from the Nutrition Chapter of my book '*The Power to Heal.*'

5. *Exercise* daily selecting walking type exercises that encourages the lymphatic system to clean up foreign invaders and take the stress off the immune system.

6. *Reduce* your exposure to chemicals through your consumer purchasing power!!! No one knows the imbalance that can result from our obsessive use of chemicals in our food, drinks, clothing, bedding, air pollution, etc., etc., etc.

7. *Understand* that body balance is impossible if your urine and saliva pH is chronically imbalanced.

EVERYTHING IN THIS GUIDEBOOK COLLECTIVELY HELPS YOUR IMMUNE SYSTEM NOT TO *GO CRAZY…AND ATTACK YOUR OWN BODY.* THIS IS WHY THE ENERGY INFORMATION IN THIS GUIDEBOOK IS SO IMPORTANT. ENJOY YOUR ENERGETIC LIFE!!!

THE MOST IMPORTANT ENERGY LESSON TO LEARN

We have reached the end of an exciting journey together. This final energy lesson popped into my head trying to go to sleep. Out of all this information this is what I want to emphasize to support your energy. **Always find the cause of your symptoms and never be willing to ONLY treat symptoms that are not life threatening, like these examples:**

1. A lady spent 10 years in a walker, but was able to walk without it in 5 days giving up allergic dairy and beef that caused her weakness. She beamed with **ENERGY** as she WALKED into my class, without her walker!

2. Many young people have been helped with a wellness program to clear up acne that affected both self-image and self-worth, causing mental and emotional stress that greatly affected their **ENERGY**.

3. Many people are treated with antibiotics for acute sinus and respiratory symptoms when the cause was viral; chemical; or allergic with molds, dust, animal danders or pollens … and not bacterial. Antibiotics set you up for unnecessary digestive problems, Candida yeast infections, and parasite overgrowth that drain you of your **ENERGY**. Antibiotics are often used to treat Lymes disease when the real problem is a suppressed immune system that antibiotics suppressed even more and that robs you of **ENERGY**.

4. One client was doubled over with left sided pain for years, but all tests … even exploratory surgery … could not find the cause. Her symptoms cleared up in 5 days off dairy and beef and she was able to regain her **ENERGY**.

5. Hundreds of my clients have been treated with out of alignment adjustments for years, when the cause was dehydration and lymphatic congestion that robbed them of their ability to enjoy life with less pain and more **ENERGY**.

6. Many people have been able to get off of antidepressants and headache medicine with correct hydration and exercise that added to their **ENERGY**.

7. Fibromyalgia and chronic fatigue can keep you in the doctor's office, but they can be turned around with the 'laws' of wellness building **ENERGY.**

8. Poor sleep is a major symptom that drains your **ENERGY,** but can often be easily corrected with the tips in this manual.

9. Chronic illness may be traced back to old mercury fillings and leaking bacteria from root canals constantly stressing the immune system, creating a loss of **ENERGY.**

10. *We have been propelled into a technological world that we have not yet learned how to live in. Many symptoms are treated with drugs without realizing the* **ENERGY** *loss from polluted frequencies.*

   These health tips were never intended to replace medical advice. I only suggest you live by the 'laws' of wellness ***long enough to make an energy difference.*** **In time**, you may be able to discuss changing or eliminating some drugs with your doctor. Be appreciative that doctors are there to treat you in an **acute situation**. Many people are getting upset with the medical profession … but remember … *if you take better care of yourself, you will not have to ask them to make you well.* **If you can find a doctor who will be there for you in a crisis, supports and contributes to rebuilding your 'energy,' you are indeed fortunate.**
   I CONGRATULATE YOU FOR COMPLETING THIS GUIDEBOOK!!!

HOLISTIC COOKBOOK

INTRODUCTION TO HEALTHY MEAL PLANNING

WELCOME TO A WORLD OF EASY AND EXCITING MEALS THAT WILL PUT SMILES ON THE FACES OF YOUR FRIENDS AND RELATIVES, MAKE YOUR FAMILY VERY HAPPY ... AND YOU VERY PROUD! I hope you will open up your culinary mold to include new ideas and taste experiences that can make life just plain more enjoyable. Learn to take a recipe 'idea' and **change it to suit your taste or medical needs.** Almost every recipe can be 'an original.' Be willing to try new ingredients. One bad meal will **not take years off your life** if you try something and do not like it. However, trying something new and liking it **can add years of enjoyment to your life** as you choose to make it again and again. **PLEASE READ EVERY RECIPE EVEN IF YOU DO NOT WANT TO FIX IT BECAUSE YOU MAY PICK UP SOME COOKING TIPS, INTERESTING FACTS, OR AN IDEA FOR 'YOUR ORIGINAL' BASED ON INGREDIENTS YOU DO LIKE.**

Some recipes may not be digested well unless you drink enough filtered and energized water throughout the day, drink ½-1 glass of water before you eat with no water during or ½ hour after the meal, and balance your pH. Make the recipes simpler, increase or decrease ingredients, or eliminate the meat if you are a vegetarian. **Anyone can adjust any recipe by substituting other ingredients to a basic idea.** Vegetarians can change any recipe using chicken broth to vegetable broth. I do not believe anyone needs to eat red meat to stay healthy, but an occasional hormone and antibiotic free egg, or ocean fish several times a week could be very helpful in balancing the diet. The healthiest fish you can eat is sardines in water. I am not an advocate of a *strict* vegetarian diet for the following reasons:

1. Vegetarians tend to eat too much fruit that feeds Candida yeast and parasites. A high fruit diet could contribute to high triglycerides that could lead to a build up of plaque in the circulatory system, increasing risks of memory loss, heart disease, male sexual problems, fatty liver, colon symptoms and fatty gut. Fresh organic fruit grown in this country should be eaten only once a day, limiting tropical fruits that are high in fructose to occasional social situations.

2. Vegetarians should consider B12 sublingual tablets, or add Spirulina to the diet.

3. Vegetarians may be more prone to a zinc deficiency, as zinc in plant food is not so

bio-available as in animal products. Zinc is a mineral found in all cells of the body, and is called a 'cofactor' because zinc is required for many normal body reactions.

4. A strict vegetarian diet is <u>high in vegetable phosphorus</u>. Excess phosphorus leaves the body as calcium phosphate, depleting calcium levels and imbalances the pH chemistry of the body. The brain needs a form of phosphorus from animal, fowl or fish that is vibrationally different than vegetable phosphorus, according to The Chemistry of Man, by Bernard Jensen.

5. Vegetarians who eat too much soy can contribute to high estrogen levels, as well as stressing the thyroid causing the <u>thyroid to be over or under active</u>. <u>High estrogen levels</u> can lead to cancer in men and women, or endometriosis and fibroids in women. The jury is still out on the health aspects of soy **so *thoroughly investigate the pros and cons of soy before deciding how much to include in your diet*.** <u>Soy is high in protein and can easily become an allergenic food if the digestive system is not healthy.</u> In some people this can lead to autoimmune diseases discussed on page 109. Infants fed soy milk can contribute to hormone and thyroid imbalance and early sexual development.

6. Even with soy and food combining vegetarians can often be <u>low in protein</u>, and <u>low energy</u>.

7. Non-strict vegetarians tend to eat a diet high in dairy products. Again, I suggest you research the pros and cons of dairy before deciding how much to consume as this could also be an <u>allergic problem</u> with symptoms anywhere in the body; and can contribute to autoimmune diseases in some people.

8. Vegetarians who are **not eating <u>organic</u>** <u>fruits, vegetable and grains</u> can have high levels of chemicals in their body that can cause stress in any part of the body, especially the liver and lymphatic system.

9. Vegetarians often eat a lot of sprouts, and they may contain mold unless washed before eating. Frequent exposure to <u>mold</u> can stress the immune system, and can be part of the stress that could lead to autoimmune diseases in some people.

SO KEEP AN OPEN MIND ... READ EVERY RECIPE ... BE CREATIVE ... AND ENJOY EASY *CULINARY ARTISTRY* IN YOUR COOKING ADVENTURE!

HOW TO MAKE A QUICK FABULOUS SALAD

FROM DORI'S KITCHEN – 1

Anyone can throw a few vegetables on lettuce and call it a salad. The title says, HOW TO MAKE A **QUICK FABULOUS** SALAD … so here are some tips.

First, start with clean, fresh organic ingredients. Wash vegetables as soon as you get home and store in large hard plastic containers. I use lock and lock containers from QVC that keeps food fresh for weeks.

Second, you need a container in the freezer of organic sunflower seeds, and pumpkin seeds. Sesame seeds have glucose lowering powers and are best kept in the freezer in a separate container since they are so small they sink to the bottom of a mix. A handful of these life saver seeds give a salad or any food added incredible crunch and *super nutritional power in a small package!*

Third, rotate tolerated items such as canned artichoke hearts, canned green chilies, green or black olives, hard boiled eggs, crumbled organic turkey bacon or your favorite ingredient. Wash organic canned beans under running water <u>until all foam is gone</u> to get rid of the indigestible sugar that causes intestinal gas, then add to salads.

Fourth, crunch gives the salad character! Besides seeds, top a salad with Terra Exotic Vegetable Stix or crumbled whole chips that adds interest and crunch. Terra chips are all root vegetables that do not state organic but are imported from other countries, or contain less chemicals than vegetables grown above ground.

Be willing to try new tolerated vegetables. These organic vegetables make great salads: Romaine or leafy lettuce, organic mixed lettuce you can buy in bulk, baby carrot, red or green pepper, radish, cucumber, yellow or green summer squash, cherry or sliced tomato, spring onion or finely chopped sweet white onion, green or red cabbage, green or black olives, or celery. *Who doesn't know that list? Have you tried adding Bok choy, Chinese cabbage, strips of raw jicama or kohlrabi (refer to Nutrition Chapter in my book), or rinsed sprouts to your salad?*

Fine chopping really helps a good salad, so purchase a special chopping knife or buy a vegetable shredder. Check kitchen stores or QVC TV programs for the latest to make kitchen work easier.

Any recipe of leftover meat, fowl, fish or seafood makes a salad a meal. If you are tired after a long day but need to stop at the grocery store, consider getting steamed shrimp and make a salad. If you do not feel well on the shrimp seasoning you can request they steam the shrimp without any seasoning and let your salad dressing at home season them. *You could even call home and ask your husband or one of the children to make the salad because you are on your way with the shrimp.* **In a family everyone works together.**

Sardines in water are low in mercury and **wins the award for nutritional excellence.** The best brand is Wild Planet in a BPA free can and low in mercury.

Moist chunks of poached wild salmon before adding the dressing makes a fabulous meal:

To poach wild salmon, cover with water and ½ teaspoon unrefined sea salt, teaspoon garlic powder, 2 teaspoons dried parsley and 2 teaspoons onion flakes. Cover with a lid and simmer 20-30 minutes. Remove any bones or skin. Toss with cooked asparagus, any cooked organic pasta shape; season to taste with melted butter, sea salt, lemon juice and dill for a delicious lunch or dinner salad.

In the end, the prize for a good salad may go to the salad dressing. Making your own could be as simple as:

- *Combining Coconut Secret Vinegar with Coconut Crystals, olive oil, Dijon mustard and sea salt.*

- *Combining Hummus with Coconut Crystals and your choice of oil.*

- *Read labels and find an organic brand that does not have ingredients you are trying to avoid.*

Learn to be creative!

COOKED VEGETABLES ADD SPARK TO A MEAL

Sometimes a meal needs color, a taste variation or something that makes the arrangement look like it belongs on the cover of a cooking magazine. Remember your seed mixture or sesame seeds browned in Better Butter recipe helps any vegetable.

CARROT RECIPES

Cook a package of baby organic carrots in a small amount of water just enough to cover, until crisp-tender. Drain, and **PLEASE drink the sweet mineral rich water.**

Combine: *2 tablespoons (or adjust to taste) Better Butter (recipe on 29)*
2 tablespoon of your favorite mustard
¼ teaspoon organic ground ginger (more or less to taste) OR ground fresh ginger, unrefined sea salt to taste, toss and accent your main course.

<u>OR</u>:   *Toss 1 lb. slivered carrots in ½ tbsp. olive oil and sea salt and roast 25 minutes. Coat carrots with 1 tbsp. Coconut Secret vinegar and ½ tbsp. low glycemic index Coconut Crystals ... roast 6-8 minutes.*

STRING BEANS OR ASPARAGUS

Cut 2 cups of fresh string beans or asparagus into 2 inch lengths, or buy organic frozen string beans or asparagus. Cook with water salted with unrefined sea salt just to cover, until tender (do not overcook). Drain and **drink the mineral rich water.**

Combine: *2 tablespoons Better Butter (or adjust to taste)*
2 large cloves fresh organic garlic (or more to taste)
¼ teaspoon organic dried basil (or more to taste)
2 tablespoons fresh organic parsley (or 1 tablespoon dried parsley)
2 teaspoons of organic lemon juice (adjust to taste)

Sea salt and pepper to taste; toss and serve. Add freshly ground pepper at the table, because cooked black pepper can produce toxic substances.

OR:
- *Broil 1 lb. fresh asparagus with 2 tbsp. olive oil and sea salt 6-8 minutes.*
- *You can also sprinkle broiled asparagus with cinnamon.*
- *Bake **very lightly** salted asparagus in a 350 degree oven until almost done. Then drizzled with olive oil and divide into equal bunches. Wrap each bunch with one slice of organic turkey bacon; broil until the bacon is crisp.*

BROCCOLI, CAULIFLOWER, ASPARAGUS, ZUCCHINI OR GREEN BEANS

*Try this cooked recipe since these vegetables are high in phytates, which if eaten raw all the time can decrease the availability of the nutrients in the food. They are all best lightly steamed except for zucchini that can be eaten raw or steamed. Cut vegetable into serving pieces and barely cover with salted (optional) water. Steam until crisp but slightly tender. Drain and **drink the mineral rich water.***

*For 2 servings **LIGHTLY** brown 2 tablespoons of organic sesame seeds in a **dry skillet on medium heat**. Add 3 tablespoons Better Butter to the seeds …melt, and pour over the vegetable in the saucepan … delectable to the palate and the eye.*

OR: *Coat with olive oil, fresh garlic, lemon juice to taste; and chopped nut choice.*

OR: *Coat with olive oil, unrefined sea salt to taste; chopped roasted nut of choice, and organic dried cranberries for a festive holiday vegetable.*

OR: *On a baking sheet toss with olive oil and sea salt. All these vegetables can be broiled 8-10 minutes, and topped with tolerated bread crumbs mixed with olive oil, and your choice of lemon juice, fresh chopped garlic, parsley, cilantro or basil.*

SERVE ANY OF THESE DELICIOUS VEGETABLES WITH A SMILE … AND REALIZE HOW EASY IT IS TO MAKE A PLAIN VEGETABLE INTO A SPECIAL VEGETABLE! <u>YOU MAY FIND FUSSY CHILDREN AND ADULTS WILLING TO EAT VEGETABLES THEY REFUSED TO EAT BEFORE.</u>

CHICKEN OR VEGETARIAN RICE BAKE

FROM DORI'S KITCHEN – 3

*For some people **every day** is fast paced … for others **some days** are too hectic.* Regardless, we all need recipes that are easy to fix or can be put together the night before, or early morning. This is a recipe that has been one of my favorites for those busy days that demands organization. Many times I have put this recipe together in the morning and stuck it in the oven just before my last client. When I'm finished working dinner is ready. If you are lucky enough to have a helper husband like I have, while I'm busy and the dinner is baking, he fixes a fabulous salad … and his salads should be a picture on the front of a magazine. If you are getting this ready in the morning remember to get the chicken out of the freezer to thaw in the refrigerator before you go to bed, and by morning it is thawed enough to make the recipe. It costs a little more, but I always buy organic skinless and boneless pieces to make it even easier. Spray all sides of a large casserole with olive oil. <u>All non-stick sprays contain soy, so if that is a problem just take a paper towel and oil the casserole with olive oil.</u> Make sure the casserole has a lid. *Combine in the casserole the following:*

- 1 very large red or yellow onion sliced (white onion is too sweet).
- 1 full cup of organic brown rice (Jasmine or Basmati are best tasting) or any combination of organic whole grain aromatic rice choices blended with Lundberg <u>Quick</u> Wild Rice that opens up and is softer than regular wild rice.
- ¼ rounded teaspoon of any or all of the following organic herbs: crumbled organic rosemary, oregano, basil, tarragon, marjoram and thyme.
- ½ cup of chopped organic celery.
- 3 very large organic garlic cloves … or 1 rounded teaspoon of organic garlic powder. You can also buy jars of fresh chopped garlic.
- 3 tablespoons of fresh parsley … or 1 tablespoon organic dried parsley.
- 1 teaspoon natural sea salt … more or less to taste.
- 3 cups of organic Imagine brand chicken broth or **No-chicken broth if you are a vegetarian.**
- 4 pieces of chicken … thighs or legs that are skinned. If you eat only white meat then use 2 chicken breasts.

— **Vegetarians add any choice of canned beans instead of chicken. Make sure you rinse the canned beans until all foam is gone.**

Stir everything well and put the covered casserole in the refrigerator until you are ready to bake it. Make sure you put a *cold casserole* in the *cold oven* to warm up as the oven preheats or you could break the container. Bake 1½ hours at 400 degrees. If the chicken contains the bone, remove chicken from the bone and stir into the mixture before serving. All cuts of chicken should be cut into pieces and stirred into the rice.

This recipe looks pale on the plate without some color. You can add color and stretch the recipe by adding ½ package frozen peas at the end. **It is the energy of color that should be a part of every meal.** Without the peas consider slightly steamed broccoli, asparagus, string beans, or bake squash in the oven at the same time as the chicken to give the plate color and interest. Spread red tomatoes on the plate or use raw finger food vegetables to brighten the plate anytime you are too rushed to make a salad.

For a quick salad add olive oil, lemon juice and chopped artichoke hearts (packed in water) with bagged organic mixed greens.

Then listen to the raves as you humbly say … *it was easy.*

HOT SALMON (OR VEGETABLE) BUNS

FROM DORI'S KITCHEN – 4

Occasionally you will put together a recipe that is just plain great … and when you add easy you have a winner. **This is an easy, nutritious and can even be called fun food. Always be on the lookout for meals that add interest to otherwise routine cooking choices.** <u>**Vegetarians can easily turn this into a hot vegetable bun.**</u>

Take three organic whole grain wheat or spelt English muffins and cut in half (or use any tolerated bread slices). Butter each half with Better Butter (recipe on 29) and lay butter side down on a pancake grill on very low heat to warm and slightly toast English muffins or use tolerated bread.

In a bowl mix together … and adjust ingredients to taste:

- *One small can of **<u>Wild Planet</u>** salmon plus unrefined sea salt to taste. You could also use canned **<u>Wild Planet</u>** Skipjack or Albacore tuna or other steamed fish, shrimp, or crab. **Wild Planet** is BPA free and lowest in mercury. You should not buy the same fish choice all the time as different locations can have different pollution levels.* <u>**Vegetarians can use hummus or beans as a base and add the rest of the ingredients.**</u>
- *One rounded teaspoon of organic dried parsley … or 1 rounded tablespoon fresh.*
- *½ rounded teaspoon of organic dried garlic … best flavor is <u>3 cloves fresh garlic</u>.*
- *Five tablespoons of finely chopped organic sweet white or red onion based on taste.* <u>**The salmon or tuna is mild so the seasonings are important.**</u>
- *Four rounded tablespoons of finely chopped organic celery (taste celery first to make sure it is not bitter).*
- *Five rounded tablespoons of organic mayonnaise.*
- *Pile on the warm, very lightly toasted buns or bread and cover with thin slices of Manchego sheep cheese that does not test allergic like dairy choices. This is an open faced sandwich and easy to eat.*
- *Warm in a 350 degree oven for 10-15 minutes to melt the cheese.*

Serve open faced on a plate with lots of colorful finger food vegetables like cherry tomatoes, slices of zucchini, green or red or yellow pepper, cucumber, baby carrots, black olives, cooked beets, celery filled with any flavored hummus from the health food store, white end of Bok Choy can be filled with any dip ... or any other veggie of choice.

This is great tasting food for a company lunch, or a casual dinner. This recipe is great for a summer meal on the patio or a sports party. If you serve it with a homemade soup one salmon bun is enough surrounded by all the beautiful vegetables ... and it makes the double recipe stretch to feed 8-10 people.

It is fun eating as a relief from the usual dinner routine. Enjoy the change from the ordinary!

**The only thing left to add is enjoyment ...
and smile from the compliments!**

OSTRICH, BUFFALO, TURKEY BACON, OR VEGAN SANDWICH

Ostrich has all the flavor of beef without the allergic reaction, is low in fat and calories, low in sodium, easier to digest and is a healthy alternative to red meat. It is available in most large health food stores, and comes in a variety of cuts. Ostrich is a good choice for a fast meal because it cooks in minutes. It looks like red meat, but it is fowl and not classified as red meat. *For a memorable meal make this easy selection:*

Put Better Butter (recipe on 29) on both halves of any organic whole grain hamburger bun or tolerated bread, and place face down on a pancake grill or large skillet. Warm on low to medium heat to slightly brown and soften.

*Cut the ostrich slices into **very thin strips**. The thinner the strips, the easier it is to eat the sandwich. Sauté in 2 teaspoons of organic extra virgin olive oil for 5 minutes, and sprinkle with natural sea salt. **If you cannot find ostrich or it costs too much, try buffalo steak. If that is also out of your budget use strips of organic turkey bacon.***

When I was a little girl I use to love tomato sandwiches, so vegans ... enjoy your version.
*Put the following on **each** half of the chosen bread:*

- *Organic mayonnaise (I prefer to keep soy at a minimum, so the best option is organic Canola) to both sides of the bun or bread.*
- *Organic relish to both sides of the bun or bread.*
- *Mustard of choice to both sides of the bun or bread. The old yellow mustard is not what it used to be. There are many different mustard flavors to try.*
- ***On one side** place very thin slices of **white or red** organic onion (white is sweetest).*
- *Thin slices of ripe organic tomato if tolerated and organic lettuce finish the sandwich beautifully.*
- *Optional: whole or diced mild green chilies you can buy in a can.*
- *Add the cooked strips to the side that does not have the onion, tomato, and lettuce, and serve open faced, letting the person close when ready to eat, because the fullness makes it topple.*
- ***Vegans use hummus or warmed refried beans.***

Place the open faced sandwich on a plate with finger food organic vegetables like slices of green or yellow summer squash, black olives, green pepper, cucumber, radish, celery, carrots or your choice. *This makes a beautiful presentation for a company lunch or an easy family dinner.* One package of ostrich meat will make 3 sandwiches.

If you cannot have any bread you can sauté seasoned ground buffalo or turkey patties instead of making a sandwich … and serve with a salad. Buffalo is a red meat and is digested better if your saliva pH is in the normal range of preferably 6.6-7.0. It is hard to tell the difference between ground buffalo burgers and beef burgers, but buffalo does <u>not</u> have the same allergic potential as beef. *The buffalo ARE coming back … in health food stores and also in some restaurants look for buffalo hamburgers or buffalo steak on the menu!*

You can choose to serve this nutritious meal with a small cup of any soup you may have made another time and frozen.

Relax … chew each bite well and enjoy …
You have done a great job of preparing healthier food!

A HEALTHY VERSION OF SEAFOOD OR VEGAN PASTA

FROM DORI'S KITCHEN – 6

*Shell fish may not contain antibiotics and hormones but they DO have another MAJOR problem …
chemicals and pollution from our bay waters.* Shell fish are bottom feeders … **need I say more**.
When I go to a restaurant I first look for an ocean fish recipe. Second choice is a crab recipe
(because of the cleaner claw meat), then other shell fish with shrimp LAST CHOICE. **Can
you guess why?** Because in a restaurant recipe shrimp may not be deveined so the toxic
levels of the shrimp may be worse.

I started buying shrimp more when health food stores started carrying eco-friendly shrimp
that are free of chemicals, raised in a state-of-the-art aquaculture facility avoiding the
pollution that is associated with shrimp farming around the globe. The shrimp are fed
organic food **and you can taste the difference!** You can get both small and medium shrimp
for all your favorite recipes from scampi to curry to skewers … or just put on a salad.

SO HOW DO YOU MAKE A HEALTHY SEAFOOD OR VEGAN PASTA MEAL?

Make a fabulous salad first, as the shrimp recipe only takes about 15-20 minutes.

*Then cook amount desired of organic whole grain pasta in salted water. Whole wheat is heavy and
chewier so whole spelt, or Tinkyada rice pasta is my preference.*

*While the pasta is cooking, you can make the sauce quickly. Amounts and taste preference varies,
so I'll just list the **organic** ingredients and you make to taste:*

1. *sauté a **large** finely chopped **white or red** onion **and lots of** fresh chopped garlic cloves (8
   cloves or more) in 3 tablespoons of olive oil until tender.*

2. *add 2 tablespoons of fresh parsley … or 1 tablespoon organic dried parsley*

3. *add 1 jar (8 oz.) of clam juice. This Crown Prince Natural Clam Juice is a product of
   Holland and is especially produced for the natural product industry. It is delicious to add
   to any fish or seafood recipe when you need more liquid. If you cannot find it check www.*

crownprince.com. *If you do not have this product add organic chicken broth or* **_vegans add Imagine brand No-chicken broth or vegetable broth._** *Add natural sea salt to taste. Adjust ingredients for more than 2-3 people.*

4. *Rinse cooked pasta and add the cleaned shrimp (or other seafood choice) to the sauce, and simmer* **2 minutes**. *DO NOT OVERCOOK!!! If you cannot find clam juice, use canned clams with juice instead of shrimp for a clam pasta meal. The organic chicken broth works well with scallops, but cut them into quarters if they are large.*

5. **_For a vegan version use no-chicken broth and stir fry veggies of choice; top pasta with finely chopped organic nuts._**

6. *Serve immediately over the pasta, with the fabulous salad you already made.*

7. *Optional over the pasta is finely shredded Manchego sheep cheese (sold in bulk way less expensive at Costco or other warehouse locations). Manchego sheep cheese can clump if heated in a stir-fry but melts easily if it is shredded fine and barely heated.*

Note: *Manchego sheep cheese also makes a great grilled cheese sandwich.*

NOW SMILE … YOU'VE EARNED ALL THE COMPLIMENTS!

GRILLED VEGETABLES

A FAVORITE PIECE OF EQUIPMENT – THE GEORGE FOREMAN GRILL COMES WITH TWO DRIP PANS FOR CONTINUOUS REBASTING.

These vegetables are the hit of any family meal or dinner party. They can be a creative person's dream placing all the colors on the platter in an eye appealing way. **This recipe makes vegetables fun food and great for company meals.**

Preheat the grill for 5 minutes and the oven to warm for storage as you remove cooked vegetables from the grill. Melt enough Better Butter (recipe on 29) with a shaker of sea salt if desired and a little garlic paste or powder to make a basting sauce for the vegetables. This may be enough for your taste *or you can omit the garlic sauce and baste with your favorite salad dressing … or top each piece after grilling with the garlic sauce mixed with a little of your favorite salad dressing.* **BE CREATIVE!**

The following are the best vegetables to grill after you have brushed both sides with your choice of basting sauce. *As each grill full of vegetables is done transfer to the oven to keep warm, and put the next group on the grill.* **The following vegetables cook in different times. Test each choice for doneness before removing from the grill:**

Three minutes: *Eggplant peeled and sliced ½ inch thick*
Very large garlic cut in half (everyone loves this, so grill a lot)
Only grill sweet white or red onions cut ½ inch thick (not yellow onions)
Green or yellow zucchini can be cut ½ inch thick, or sliced lengthwise.
The trick to grilling vegetables is that all vegetables on the grill at the same time be the SAME THICKNESS for uniform cooking.

Two minutes: *Mushrooms of choice should be* **same thickness** *of ½ inch*
Green, yellow or red peppers … cut off the ends to lie flat, and use the cut off pieces the next day in a stir-fry or omelet.

One minute: *Tomatoes should be cooked separately and sliced about ½ inch thick.*

Spread out on a platter these vegetables transform any main course meal into a color splash. **Remember ... color is energy ... and energy runs your life!**

Or ... **be creative** and stuff the grilled vegetables into whole grain pita bread, or top them over organic pasta or rice. Spread with your favorite salad dressing or organic mayonnaise and shredded lettuce on your tolerated bread for a delicious grilled vegetable sandwich. Optional addition is shredded Manchego sheep cheese. If you want a protein with this fun meal add the health food store version of organic chicken nuggets or fish sticks. These tidbits can also be heated on the grill in *half the time it takes in the oven because the heat is pressed onto both sides ...* also grill fish, buffalo or ostrich burgers.

**If you want a 'fast' best friend buy a George Foreman Grill, and ...
ENJOY NUTRITIOUS, QUICK AND EASY MEALS!**

FABULOUS MACARONI CHICKEN DINNER

FROM DORI'S KITCHEN – 8

This recipe is simple to make … freezes well … and is wickedly delicious.

Thin slice two organic skinless chicken breasts, or 4-6 skinless and boneless thighs; remember to wash your hands, counter or cutting board and knife well after touching raw chicken. Sauté with:

- *a large organic white or red onion thinly sliced (they are sweeter than yellow onions)*
- *two teaspoons of organic garlic powder (4 chopped garlic cloves if you have time)*
- *two tablespoons of organic dried parsley (or 4 tablespoons chopped fresh)*
- *one teaspoon of natural sea salt (or adjust to taste)*
- *add one quart of organic chicken broth after mild browning of the chicken and onions.*

You can either cook on top of the stove for 30-45 minutes, or if you do not have time to check on it occasionally, stick it in the oven at 400 degrees for one hour.

Cook 2 cups of organic elbow macaroni (whole wheat, spelt, or Tinkyada rice pasta that holds together and tastes like wheat pasta) or any other shape of organic whole grain pasta cooked in salted water until almost tender … rinse and drain. If you have never tried Tinkyada rice pasta that has award winning taste and texture, check your health food store. If they do not have it research on line at www.tinkyada.com.

Add the pasta that <u>needs a little more cooking</u> back into the stock mixture. Cook together until tender. For the secret ingredient and the taste of a 'sour crème sauce', add 4 tablespoons of organic canola mayonnaise for a different taste treat. Not everyone approves of canola products but I prefer canola over soy mayonnaise for the few times you need a mayonnaise. You can also check the internet for the Ener-G Egg Free Mayonnaise recipe you can make at home without canola, soy or eggs.

Serve in a soup bowl with one of your super salad combinations, or a pile of organic raw finger vegetables.

131

Leftovers warm up well the second day for lunch or dinner, but this recipe also freezes well if a single person likes to make recipes for multiple meals. If you do have leftovers they should be consumed in one to two days unless frozen.

A purist will find fault with starch and protein together but the American diet is full of sandwiches, pastas, rice and potato recipes. Perfect food combining makes it difficult *given the attitude about recipes in modern America.* **However, if you are ill you may need to consider eating better food combining for improved digestion. For most people** *understanding the importance of correct pH for good digestion, drinking the correct amount of energized water based on your body weight, drinking a glass of water before each meal and none with the meal or ½ hour after the meal, improving your ability to* **control stress in your life and at mealtime,** *and research products that protect you from the draining stress of modern technology . . . will all help digestion.*

Read the Digestion Chapter in my book 'The Power to Heal.' For the beginning health student the recipes provided in this manual are at least healthier versions of old time less healthy favorites . . . it is a place to start!

So, check your saliva pH ... drink your energized water before meals ... chew your food well ... relax ... and enjoy your organic food.

Life is good!

HEALTHY SAUSAGE

The very word 'sausage' strikes fear in the hearts of health minded people. Oh no, not hard to digest fatty pork that could be from unhealthy animals, full of hormones, antibiotics and who knows what drugs. Well, people who make healthy food choices can now have sausage thanks to Blackwing Ostrich Meats. Their gourmet quality ostrich sausage patties have all the delicious flavor of beef … yet is 94% less fat and 54% fewer calories than chicken. They are 98% fat free, yet high in protein, and have mild seasoning. Blackwing ostrich are alfalfa and corn fed and graze on free range pastures. Prepare the same as beef or pork sausage in any recipe. If you cannot find this product call 1-800-326-7874.

You can make your own sausage from organic ground chicken, turkey, buffalo, ostrich, or emu by adding sea salt and ground sage to taste.

Ways you can use ostrich sausage, or your own sausage:

- *Crumble and add to any tomato sauce over your favorite pasta.*

- *Serve with your favorite egg preparation as a side dish for breakfast or brunch, and your favorite whole grain toast with Better Butter (recipe on 29).*

- *Makes a delicious sandwich with all the fixings like organic lettuce, organic mayonnaise, organic relish, mustard of choice, sliced organic white or red onion and sliced organic tomato on organic sprouted whole grain bread.*

- *Great as part of a mixture that goes into an omelet, along with sweet white onions.*

- *Add to stuffing in chicken or turkey (stuffing can also be baked on the side).*

- *Make a stuffing and lay **under** a whole turkey breast you can purchase as turkey parts in many health food stores. **Top** turkey breast with a sliced white onion and bake **covered** in the oven at 350 degrees for about 1 ½ hours, or until turkey is done. Be creative … changing what covers the turkey changes the whole recipe.*

- *Good cold left over in the refrigerator for a quick protein snack.*

- *Good covered with hummus you can buy ready made in health food stores.*

- *Can be crumbled after cooking and add to a large salad that can be the main meal for a lunch or a hot summer evening.*

- *Can be crumbled after cooking and used instead of beef in tacos or pita bread*

- *Can be crumbled after cooking and be part of the ingredients in a Quesadilla. A press that makes Quesadillas is another must have kitchen cookware.*

- *Can be crumbled after cooking and layered with diced organic tomatoes, chopped white organic onion, organic mayonnaise, organic relish and organic sprouts rolled up in a soft whole grain tortilla ... or a Romaine lettuce leaf.*

Get the message ... you think of some other ways. One of the best things about ostrich sausage is the delicate seasoning ... it is not hot with a bite ... just good tasting! <u>If it is still too seasoned for you, boil in water before adding to above suggestions to wash off some of the seasoning.</u>

<u>**Remember, ostrich or emu is not red meat; and emu eggs are different than chicken eggs for allergies.**</u> *You can get Emu meat, eggs, 1ˢᵗ aid and cosmetic products in your area if you Google for your local sources.*

ENJOY!!!

THE HEALTHY HOT DOG

What has happened to the good old American hot dog? We eat approximately 60 hot dogs per person in the U.S. ... that is two billion pounds of hot dogs a year! Every part of the country has its favorite hot dog that can range from beef, pork, chicken, turkey, buffalo, and deer dogs (you supply the deer). Hot dogs started out in Frankfurt, Germany in 1652 and were served to customers along with white gloves to hold them. Since the gloves were not always returned to the concessionaires, one man teamed up with a local baker to create the hot dog roll just to protect the fingers of his customers.

Unfortunately, the hot dog has gone to the dogs. There are horror stories about the quality, even disease condition of some of the animals used to make commercial hot dogs. They added hormones, antibiotics and drugs to the animals and fowl, and feed them food full of chemicals so **the prized hot dog has become a nightmare food.** To add insult to injury they are served on buns that are *low nutrition and high in chemicals.*

How do you make a prize winning, applause producing, healthy hot dog meal?

1. *Cut an organic whole grain bun like wheat, spelt, or rice you can find in all health food stores in half and spread a thin layer of Better Butter on each half. Place butter side down on a pancake grill to* **lightly toast on low heat***. If you cannot find tolerated buns, use tolerated bread including millet in the same way. If you cannot tolerate any bread top the hot dog with options below and eat with a fork.*

2. *Next, cut the* **organic** *chicken, turkey, or buffalo hot dog in half (pork is too hard to digest, beef is hard to digest and can be allergic and soy may or may not be tolerated). Remove buns from the grill, split hot dogs in half lengthwise, and lightly toast in a little Better Butter, turning once. You can choose to boil them in water, and split them to lay flat on the bun.*

3. *While the hot dogs are warming, spread these options on each side of the buns:*

   - *organic mayonnaise and/or organic catsup.*
   - *organic relish like pickle relish or corn relish.*

- or mix mayo, relish and ½ ripe avocado or hummus for a great spread.
- add one of the many organic mustard flavored products of choice.

Optional additions to the buns:

- diced chili peppers or diced tomatoes.
- very thin sliced or finely diced white or red onions (not yellow onions).
- shredded lettuce (try using up the tops of Bok Choy).
- shredded Manchego sheep cheese.
- organic sauerkraut; left over coleslaw; refried beans or left over beans.

Serve the option topped hot dogs (<u>with or without the bun</u>) with <u>any finger food vegetable choice or</u> Terra exotic vegetable chips.

Without the bun serve with oven baked sweet potatoes peeled and cut into 1 inch pieces, coated with olive oil, sea salt and sprinkled with thyme. Baked at 400 degrees for 1 hour (or buy precut organic sweet potatoes and bake according to directions). If tolerated precut and frozen 'Oven Reds' are organic red potatoes that are better digested than white potatoes. Keep in mind that red potatoes are in the nightshade family but sweet potatoes are not. People with joint problems may tolerate sweet potatoes better then red potatoes.

Enjoy your nutritious fun food!

IDEAS FOR BREAKFAST

When you start to eat healthier, breakfast is often the hardest meal of the day to figure out what to eat. Some people are at a loss after finding out that coffee, a donut or their favorite cereal with cow's milk is not a good choice. **Consider the following ...**

– *Cut up a serving of organic fruit of choice into* **small** *pieces. Best choices are American grown fruits that are lower in fructose than tropical fruits. Make a mix of organic sunflower seeds and pumpkin seeds to keep in the freezer and add to breakfast fruit. Add fructose free Stevia or Coconut Crystals to sweeten and non-dairy milk that can* **hold your hunger for hours.**

– *Put any organic nut butter or peanut butter on organic apple or pear wedges.*

– *If you cannot have fruit, toast your tolerated bread and spread with Better Butter, peanut butter or other nut butters plus a selection of extra nuts later for a snack. If you cannot tolerate peanut butter look for the delicious organic nut butters from Tierra Farm. The Maple Cashew Butter or Maple Pecan Butter are made in a peanut free facility and can be a wonderful substitute for the stronger flavor people enjoy in peanut butter. If you cannot find these products in your health food store check www.tierrafarm.com.*

– *Cook organic cereal like Quinoa, Oatmeal, or Cream of Rice.* **If you like cooked cereals,** *but do not have the time to eat at home, you can make the cereal* **very thin** *by adding extra non-dairy milk, and sweeten with Stevia or Coconut Crystals. Put in a pint jar to drink in the car at red lights or stop signs.*

– *Whole grain dry cereals have more loss of nutrients than cooked cereals. Since you do not always have time to cook cereal, everyone should have* **one favorite organic box cereal choice** *for* <u>occasional</u> *use. My favorite is Arrowhead Mills Maple Buckwheat Flakes. It is whole grain, organic, gluten free, and sweetened with organic sugars. With added seed mixture and organic rice milk I'm satisfied for hours. These flakes add sweetening to trail mix without the mold you get with dried fruit, and are delicious out of the box as a quick snack.*

– Goat (not goat cheese or milk), sheep, rice, and coconut yogurt (contains fat and sugar so consume only 1 x week) all test non-allergic. You can sweeten plain yogurt with the sugars listed above and add seed mix and sesame seeds.

– My best recommendation is the Blender Drink on 41. I make a quart blender drink for myself and another quart for my husband. I divide each quart drink in half for breakfast and half for lunch at least 5 days a week. This gives us both nutrition plus a way of resting the digestive system. It takes me about 10 minutes to make two meals for two people. **How long does it take you to make two meals for two people packed full of easy to digest organic nutrients?**

– Waffles made with the gluten-free Namaste brand mix available in health food stores is easy to fix by following directions on the box and topping with Better Butter, maple syrup (low glycemic index of 54) or Coconut Crystals (very low glycemic index of 35).

– **_For a great weekend breakfast for 2 people made gluten free easy to digest Quinoa pancakes:_**

> Whip 2 egg whites until stiff. In a separate bowel beat together until smooth 2 egg yolks, 1 cup Quinoa flour, 1 cup any tolerated non-dairy milk or water, ½ teaspoon natural sea salt, 2 teaspoons aluminum free baking powder, 1 tablespoon sesame oil and 1 tbsp. organic maple syrup or Coconut Nectar to help brown pancakes. Fold in egg whites and bake on a heated griddle. Serve with Better Butter and organic maple syrup or Coconut Nectar. **_If you are allergic to eggs you can substitute 2 tablespoon sprouted flaxseed and 6 tablespoons of water; increase baking powder to 1 tablespoon._**

– French toast make with your tolerated bread dipped in a mixture of eggs, non-dairy milk, natural sea salt and cinnamon, browned on a grill and topped with Better Butter and organic maple syrup or Coconut Nectar. **_If you are allergic to eggs substitute 2 tablespoons sprouted flaxseed and a little extra milk._**

NEVER SKIP BREAKFAST ... EAT SOMETHING!!!

Try running your car without gas!

**Now that you've started your day healthfully ...
have a great one!**

WAYS TO FIX THE INCREDIBLE, EDIBLE EGG

FROM DORI'S KITCHEN — 12

Except a few specialty pans, most of my cooking pans are all stainless steel, Corning ware or glass. I use cast iron in the oven, but only on my flat stove top if the outside is coated with ceramic. My cookware is Kitchen Craft Stainless Steel Cookware by West Bend, sold at health expos and fairs. I LOVE EACH PIECE … and they still look like new! For more information call 352-483-7600, or www.COOKFORLIFE.com.

SCRAMBLED EGGS

Have you ever made scrambled eggs that were dry and crumbly and stuck to the pan? Here are some tricks to make delicious scrambled eggs that slide out of the pan.

__Heavily spray the bottom and sides of a heavy duty stainless steel skillet with a non-stick olive oil spray.__ On medium heat melt 1 tablespoon Better Butter for each egg going into the pan. In a small bowl __whip__ the number of eggs desired with 1 tablespoon of a non-dairy milk per egg, and natural sea salt to taste. Add eggs to the pan and stir as needed until done for soft and delicious scrambled eggs that slip out of the pan. Add shredded Manchego sheep cheese on the plate for added flavor and nutrition.

EGG OMELETS

Do you hesitate to make omelets at home because it seems like too much trouble? This is a culinary delight, and if you are looking for raves this choice for brunch, lunch or dinner will assure that. *__The egg base is a chef's secret:__*

Take a 12 inch skillet and spray with olive oil non-stick spray. New no stick coatings are not as bad a health issue as the old ones and I do have a 12 inch omelet pan I got from QVC that I love! Whip 4 eggs thoroughly with 4 tablespoons of water and natural sea salt to taste. Place eggs in the __cold pan, cover__ and put on __LOW__ heat for 15 minutes or more to __SET not to cook, so do not stir.__ Sprinkle shredded Manchego sheep cheese or Water buffalo mozzarella over ½ the eggs to melt while they are setting.

Create your filling from **ANY OF THE FOLLOWING OPTIONS or your own idea**. *Sauté your choices in olive oil until soft …*

- *finely chopped organic white or red onions are best because they are milder.*
- *finely chopped organic garlic or fresh garlic in the jar.*
- *finely chopped organic green, yellow or red peppers; green or black olives.*
- *finely chopped organic parsley (or dried), organic celery, Chinese cabbage.*
- *finely chopped organic green or yellow zucchini, or leaves from Bok Choy.*
- *finely chopped leftover organic baked red or sweet potato … or mushrooms.*
- *chopped up precooked organic turkey bacon, turkey ham or ostrich sausage.*
- *finely chopped organic tomato, corn or tomato salsa.*
- *organic chicken broth or Imagine brand No-chicken broth to add moisture.*
- *left over meat, fowl, fish, seafood or beans.*
- *your favorite mustard makes many recipes a winner.*

Pile your **CULINARY CREATION** onto ½ of the set egg and flip over the other ½ of the egg. *Cut in half while in the skillet,* and carefully lift out onto the plate with an **oversized spatula or 2 spatulas**. *Optional, sprinkle paprika or chili powder over the top of the egg for color, and* **serve with pride … and some finger food veggies!**

HARD COOKED EGGS

Have you ever hard boiled eggs that ended up with rubbery whites, the yolks a grayish yellow and a green ring between the yolk and the white. You wonder what happened to your healthy organic eggs. What happened is how you cooked them. The following guidelines will give you a beautiful tender egg that is what it should look like … yellow in the middle and pure white around the yellow center:

Temperature makes all the difference in boiling an egg. The white part of the egg cooks faster than the yellow yolk, so by the time the yolk is cooked the white is tough. If the egg stays over heat too long after cooking is complete sulfur in the white will react with the iron in the yolk and create that greenish ring. So … how do you fix it? The trick is to heat the eggs gradually covering them with an inch of cold water. When the water reaches a full boil, remove from heat and cover the pan allowing the eggs to sit in the water for 10 minutes. This cooks them slowly and prevents the whites from toughing. You can peel and use the eggs at this point, or if you are storing them you should put them in ice water to stop the heat. This lowers the temperature and reduces the pressure that causes the green rings to form. A hard-boiled egg cooked correctly tastes a lot different than one that is cook incorrectly.

DEVILED EGGS

Most people have eaten a deviled egg at a picnic and rave about how good they taste. The problem is not that we can't make them … the problem is we do not make them often enough. I use to have hard-boiled eggs in the refrigerator until I had to throw a few out. However, I have never had to throw out a deviled egg. Now, when I hard-boil a dozen eggs I made three at a time into split deviled eggs and put them in a closed container in the refrigerator. They disappear without any problem. When they are gone, I fix three more. My husband looks for the tasty deviled eggs instead of me trying to figure out what to do with the hard-boiled eggs. You should not need a summer picnic to enjoy them.

It is not difficult to make a deviled egg by mashing the yolk with mayonnaise or yogurt, maybe relish and sea salt. After you pile the mixture back into the egg white you can top with a sprinkle of paprika to give them color and a little different taste.

EGG SUBSTITUTES

Some people with an egg allergy can eat duck or emu eggs. You will have to do some local research to find your source. The best substitute I've found for eggs in cooking is:

- *1 tablespoon of organic sprouted flaxseed plus 1 tablespoon of water for each egg in the recipe.*

(OR) *You can Google egg free mayonnaise and find a recipe using Ener-G Egg Replacer but know that it does contain potato starch for people who do not tolerate nightshade foods.*

The following are ways you may be able to tolerate occasional eggs in cooking better:

- *If your saliva pH is 6.6 or above to no more than 7.2, you are hydrated with energized water and you drink a glass of water before you eat but none with the meal or ½ hour after the meal you will tolerate the protein in eggs better.*

- *Drinking a glass of water before you start to eat extracts the hydrochloric acid from the lining of the stomach to activate the protein enzyme pepsin.*

- *You also may tolerate eggs or any protein food if you do not eat it any more often than every four days so your body can clear of that food.*

HEALTHY TREATS

I do not care how healthy you want your diet to be we all like a snack food treat occasionally. Make organic popcorn and add natural sea salt and Better Butter. There is no such thing as a guilt free sweet treat, but if you have a healthy version on hand you can indulge occasionally if you need an energy boost. **Many of your favorite dessert or snack recipes can be adjusted with healthier ingredients and still enjoyed.**

I make a healthy, nutritious and organic treat that is a fabulous non-bake brownie. It is a very easy treat to make for a family snack, a gift or party:

1. *Melt 1 stick of organic butter*
2. *Add 1 cup of low glycemic index Coconut Crystals*
3. *Add ¼ cup unsweetened cocoa (or you could use carob powder)*
4. *Add ¼ cup rice milk or any tolerated non-dairy milk, and boil for 1 minute.*
5. *Add ¾ cup organic peanut butter (or any tolerated nut butter) until melted.*
6. *Stir in 3 cups organic oats (or 2 ¾ cups Quinoa for gluten free)*
7. *Add ¾ cup organic peanuts (or any other tolerated chopped nut choice)*
8. *Add 1 tsp. organic vanilla.*
9. *Spread and flatten on an oiled cookie sheet and cool in refrigerator, then cut into pieces and store in refrigerator in a sealed container until ready to eat.*

Namaste Foods from a health food store is free of allergens, and has a Brownie and Blondie mix you can add organic ingredients for a faster version.

Non-bake nut balls give an energy boost (double for a party treat):

1. *Measure one cup of organic crunchy peanut butter or other tolerated nut butter.*
2. *Add: ½ cup of Coconut Nectar.*
3. *Add: one cup of organic raisins, or chopped dates or figs. The dried fruit holds the balls together. If you have a problem with raisins, mold, or sweet snacks, you can substitute four tablespoons Quinoa flour (or other tolerated flour), and ½ cup of chopped organic nuts. **Another way some people with mold sensitivity tolerate dried fruit like raisins,***

dates, and figs is to wash dried fruit thoroughly to flush off the mold, and dry before adding to a recipe.

4. *Add: one teaspoon of organic vanilla.*
5. *Wash your hands so you can mix the dough like bread. Take your rings off, and put a little oil on your hands so the mixture sticks less to your fingers. Form balls about the size of a quarter, and roll in organic coconut. If you do not like coconut, roll balls in finely ground nut of choice.* **BE CREATIVE … THIS RECIPE CAN BE CHANGED TO BE YOUR PERSONAL FAVORITE SNACK!** *Place on a cookie sheet in the refrigerator to chill. Store in the refrigerator in a tightly closed container, for those special moments or unexpected guests.*

Who does not love a classic fudge recipe? Unfortunately, we associate fudge with sugar and dairy. You CAN make any dark <u>semi-sweet</u> fudge recipe healthier with the following changes:

1. *Melt on very low heat 100% cacao all natural unsweetened chocolate baking bar. The best tasting one I've tried is Ghirardelli brand.*
2. *Add one can of regular Coconut milk (not Lite).*
3. *Sweeten with 12 tablespoons of Coconut Crystals and ½ teaspoon of Stevia (the regular measuring ½ teaspoon and not the scoop in the jar).*
4. *Add 1 tablespoon of organic vanilla.*
5. *Add 1 cup of chopped walnuts or chopped nut of choice.*
6. *Pour into a glass baking dish and refrigerate until cool enough to cut into pieces. If this recipe does not set up enough it can be eaten as a thick pudding or put over Coconut Bliss (soy and dairy free) ice cream.*

Another <u>healthy</u> version of an old favorite is root beer floats. You can <u>upgrade</u> root beer to <u>all natural</u> versions in the health food stores. The brand I like best is Virgil's that has all natural gluten free ingredients. Put Rice Dream ice cream (or Soy Delicious ice cream if allowed, or Bliss brand of coconut ice cream if soy not tolerated) in it for a treat that brings back memories. THIS IS NOT A LOW CALORIC RECOMMENDATION BUT IS A HEALTHIER OPTION FOR A HOT SUMMER DAY OR A SPECIAL PARTY TREAT. *Again, we all need healthier treats.*

Keep organic <u>Natural Choice brand of sorbets</u> on hand for a fast treat.

Enjoy your healthy treat occasionally because you have been really good!

EASY SOUP IDEAS

This easy to make soup is a wonderful hot accompaniment to any sandwich meal. Try it for a taste treat and a fabulous food choice that gives you wonderful nutrition. **Learn to pick new foods that give your body a lot of nutrition for the effort of cooking.** *This soup will do that.* It is a rich tasting soup, so a small cup is enough added to the meal. **Do not be afraid to stretch your taste buds, and try new foods and flavors.** Most people are in a terrible rut when it comes to food choices and they miss so many wonderful experiences. <u>**I make many recipes I do not like, but my favorites would never have been discovered if I had not been willing to stretch my culinary taste buds and try something new.**</u> If you like pumpkin pie...try this soup:

In 1 teaspoon of organic virgin olive oil sauté ½ large **white or red** *onion (they are milder) with one large sprig of finely chopped organic parsley (or dried parsley) until soft. This soup is blended in a blender, so the size of the vegetables is not important.*

Stir in: *1 can of organic pumpkin*
3 tbsp. organic spelt flour that is easier to digest than wheat (Quinoa flour for gluten intolerance); blend in ⅓ cup organic Rice Dream milk (or almond).
½ LEVEL (not rounded) teaspoon of organic ground ginger. Some people may find the ginger too strong, so use ¼ level teaspoon of ginger and taste. Some people may not like the taste of ginger at all, so try cinnamon or nutmeg or pumpkin pie mix to your taste, and it will taste like liquid pumpkin pie. <u>***The seasoning can be adjusted so do not throw the baby out with the bath water.***</u>

Add: *1 ⅔ cups of non-dairy milk choice (total 2 cups), and 1 qt. organic chicken broth or* **No-chicken broth for vegetarians.**

Heat on low heat until thickened (this is a thin soup). Blend in a blender until smooth and serve in a small mug. This tastes good with any sandwich you make for lunch or dinner.

If you like this recipe it is worth making 2-3 times the amount the next time, so you can freeze for future quick additions to a meal or a conversation drink for guests. Some days you may have a few extra minutes to have **fun with cooking**, but other days you only have time for a simple effort. **This is where cooking a recipe you like 2 or 3 times and freezing gives you special treats when there is not enough time in the day.**

OR: *Add a can of organic pumpkin to any soup recipe for a delightful change of taste and added nutrition if a recipe just needs 'something'. Pumpkin is not just for the holidays!*

OR: *Buy Imagine brand organic soup like Butternut Squash; use as a meal addition or add to blender drinks. Pacific brand all natural Cashew Carrot Ginger is delicious from the box, but for more nutrition blend in a can of organic sweet potatoes in a blender before heating for a taste change. These soups make fast delicious additions to any meal, as a quick meal, or just a snack.*

OR: *Pacific brand organic French Onion soup is fabulous topped with shredded Manchego sheep cheese and organic croutons (regular or gluten free) for a quick lunch.*

OR: ***It is very hard to mess up soup.*** *You can low heat brown any meat choice with a large onion in olive oil and add celery, carrots, parsley, garlic, sea salt, herbs of choice, chicken or non-chicken broth as a base. From there add any vegetable you like (or want to clean up) to make a flavorful dinner. Soup is a good way to clean up an assortment of canned food you have been ignoring in the cupboard … or frozen food you need to move along from the freezer.*

<u>Congratulations … you've just been creative!</u>

DESSERT RECIPES

I guess by now you realize I like to use pumpkin in my cooking. I love the color, the texture, the taste and the nutrition.

PUMPKIN PUDDING

The following <u>Pumpkin Pudding</u> is so easy to fix. Baked in single serving Corning ware custard cups it makes a *great dessert* with a dab of any non-dairy ice cream, or warm pecan sauce recipe on top.

1. *Beat well, 2 medium organic eggs (not large eggs)*

2. *Add and beat together thoroughly:*

   - *1 cup of organic canned pumpkin (1 whole can fills 8 custard cups if you double all ingredients; or fill 4 custard cups with this recipe and use left over pumpkin the next night for dinner, seasoned with the Better Butter and cinnamon).*
   - *¾ cup of organic original rice or almond milk*
   - *¼ cup organic maple syrup or Coconut Nectar*
   - *2-3 teaspoons of pumpkin pie spice based on taste*
   - *½ teaspoon natural sea salt (or adjust to taste)*

3. *Put into individual corning ware type casseroles. Bake 450 degrees for 15 minutes, then 350 for 25 minutes (no longer). Best served at room temperature.*

PECAN SAUCE

<u>*Lightly*</u> *brown ½ cup coarsely chopped pecans in 2 tablespoons of organic butter.*

Add ¼ cup organic maple syrup or Coconut Nectar plus 2 tablespoons water and **simmer a few minutes until it thickens.** *This can be made the day before needed, but it must be warmed, and then poured over pumpkin custard cups. Pecan Sauce* is a big hit over any non-dairy ice cream; pumpkin pudding or pumpkin pie. For economy, because whole organic pecans are expensive, you can cut back a little on the pecans, and double the sweetener and water. I do not recommend you buy pecan pieces (or any nut pieces) because broken nuts turn rancid faster.

PUMPKIN PIE

The simplest **PUMPKIN PIE in the world** is made with purchased whole wheat, spelt, or rice crust (for gluten intolerant) that you can buy in health food stores, along with canned organic pumpkin pie filling. If you like a stronger spicy flavor, add extra nutmeg and cinnamon… or pumpkin pie spice. Follow the directions on the jar, except I use Thai Kitchen organic 'lite' coconut milk instead of evaporated milk or half and half. This version can also be baked in custard cups for a pumpkin pudding dessert. **If you cannot decide between pumpkin pie and pecan pie, try drizzling pecan sauce over your pumpkin pie … oh my that's good!**

GRAPEFRUIT SORBET

GRAPEFRUIT SORBET is easy to make if you purchase **fresh squeezed** grapefruit juice in the dairy case. If I need an easy dessert I simply combine ½ cup of fresh grapefruit juice and ¾ cup of a low glycemic Coconut Crystals in a saucepan until sugar is dissolved. Add remaining 2 ½ cup grapefruit juice and taste for sweetness as grapefruit can vary. Chill in a covered freezer-safe container and then freeze for one hour or until firm. A refreshing palate cleanser for six people after a delicious meal.

ADJUST YOUR FAVORITE DESSERT RECIPE INSTEAD OF LOOKING FOR A NEW HEALTHIER RECIPE. You can change any recipe using low glycemic flour for refined wheat flour, Coconut Crystals or Nectar for sugar and Coconut milk for dairy milk. Make all ingredients natural or organic.

It is so easy to get smiles and praises for your effort!

SIX WAYS TO ENJOY LEFT OVER CHICKEN

FROM DORI'S KITCHEN – 16

*One of the best ways to make multiple meals so you do not have to cook from scratch **every night** is to roast a chicken.* Some health food stores sell hormone and antibiotic free rotisserie chicken … or … roast your own … or two at one time for future meals. Sometimes I love to roast an old fashioned chicken by rubbing the cavity with salted Better Butter and fill with a fabulous stuffing I make from scratch with …

- *cubed toasted organic tolerated bread softened with organic chicken broth.*

- *seasoning like organic sage, marjoram, oregano, rosemary, basil, thyme, parsley, garlic and sea salt to personal taste*

- *added chopped organic celery, and onion; then stuff the chicken and enjoy the 1st meal with a salad. You should have some left over chicken if you bought the largest chicken in the case … or you can roast a second plain chicken with the stuffed one; or rotisserie (easy to buy now) 2 chickens.*

Here are some easy next day meal ideas … or freeze chicken in packages for future meals. Never eat left-over food in the refrigerator longer than 1-2 days, because of the mold growth.

- *Quickly stir fry thin strips of <u>fresh</u> chicken breasts, or stir-fry <u>cooked</u> chicken with whatever you want.*

- *Wrap chicken, chopped tomatoes, shredded non-allergenic Manchego sheep cheese and your favorite organic salsa in an organic whole wheat or corn tortilla, or pita bread. Or, make a delicious chicken sandwich.*

- *Make a version of a Reuben using organic rye bread (or any tolerated bread); sliced chicken, sliced white or red onion, organic sauerkraut, shredded Manchego cheese (good) or sliced Water Buffalo mozzarella (best). Put open faced sandwich in a 400 degree oven to melt the cheese.*

— *Add chopped chicken to other salad ingredients; add seeds or chopped nuts.*

— *Heat finely chopped chicken in organic barbecue sauce and serve on a warmed whole grain organic bun, pita bread, wheat or rice soft tortilla.*

— *Sauté finely chopped chicken with sliced organic onions, garlic, and organic cubed red potatoes, natural sea salt, and finely chopped green pepper at the end of cooking. You can moisten hash with a little organic chicken broth.*

— *Make egg drop soup with chopped chicken, organic chicken broth, lots of sliced scallions, chopped celery, whipped organic eggs added slowly, natural sea salt and garlic to taste … or add cooked rice for chicken rice soup. . . or organic whole wheat, spelt, or rice noodles for noodle soup.*

LEARN TO BE A CLEVER COOK! If you cook any ocean fish, cook double and the next night make a fabulous fish salad for dinner. Leftover meat like chicken, lamb or buffalo can be made into a stir-fry with lots of onions, garlic, parsley, vegetables like zucchini/broccoli/Chinese cabbage/Bok Choy, organic chicken broth, try various mustards, natural sea salt … *or your own idea.* I make omelets with left over turkey bacon or other left over protein from the night before. You can also season left over protein and add to an organic Taco shell with Manchego sheep cheese and finely chopped lettuce.

So remember, **COOK SMART** and <u>**let last nights left over food be the inspiration for a brand-new meal tonight**</u> **… AND HAVE EXTRA TIME FOR THE THINGS YOU WANT TO DO!**

SCOTCH BROTH

The purpose of this recipe is to acquaint you with a <u>slow cooker</u> that should be in everyone's kitchen. I start many meals in the morning and dinner is ready when I finish in the evening. My slow cooker is stainless steel from my West Bend collection I told you about, and I love it! I'll make this recipe on a weekend and cook the lamb shanks on Saturday, then refrigerator overnight so any fat is hardened to skim off. The next day I finish the easy Sunday evening dinner.

You can also use a **<u>pressure cooker</u>** that is another favorite cooking utensil I love, and cook the lamb shanks for 30 minutes. **<u>Every kitchen should have a pressure cooker and a slow cooker!</u>** It is hard to find a pressure cooker without the Teflon coating anymore. Current Teflon is supposed to be harder, safer and more scratch resistant than before (we can only hope).

This recipe has been in my file for over 40 years and I never regret the decision to make it. You do not have to be a lover of lamb to enjoy this dish. You can use lamb shanks that give it flavor without adding any lamb meat like a beef shank flavors vegetable soup; or substitute buffalo shanks from Twin Springs Farm 1-410-239-4103. Imported hormone and antibiotic free lamb from Costco is your best buy.

*So, let's start the cooking process. This is a large amount perfect for freezing so you can have a few quick easy meals in the future. **If you want to try the recipe first, you can cut all ingredients in half.** I bet you double it next time! In a slow cooker, simmer 4 organic lamb shanks in two quarts of organic chicken broth. If you prefer more meat add several inexpensive shoulder chops. When cooked remove the meat from the bone and add to the broth. Refrigerate overnight or sit in the garage overnight in the cold winter. Skim the fat from the broth ... then add the following:*

- *another two quarts of organic chicken broth*
- *2 large red or yellow organic onions (white onions makes it too sweet)*
- *3 full stalks of chopped organic celery and 1 cup of diced organic carrots*
- *½ cup of chopped fresh organic parsley or 2 tablespoons organic dried*
- *4 minced large garlic cloves or ½ tablespoon organic dried garlic*

- 2 teaspoons of natural sea salt (adjust to taste after all ingredients are cooked)
- 2 cups of uncooked whole grain rice; or you can substitute a 10 oz package of cut okra, and 1 cup of organic barley for a different taste
- 2 teaspoons each of organic dried marjoram, dried thyme and dried rosemary
- 6 bay leaves that **must be removed at the end of cooking**
- 4 medium cubed organic red potatoes with eyes removed but unpeeled
- optional: 2 small chopped turnips (larger, older turnips can be bitter). Extra turnips make a good substitute if potatoes are not tolerated.
- optional: ½ package of frozen organic baby peas or canned organic black eyed peas with the foam completely rinsed off.

Simmer at low boil for one hour, or until everything is cooked. Remove the 6 bay leaves and adjust the taste as needed. **Serve with a fabulous salad … and freeze the rest. This is a perfect hardy winter meal. You can always change the ingredients to make it YOUR favorite recipe.**

<u>Whenever you can cook more than one meal at a time for future easy meals … that recipe is a winner!</u>

BOUILLABAISSE

I love to work with this recipe. I make **<u>4 times the base recipe</u>** and freeze the stock. *Then when I want a quick meal I thaw some stock, bring to a boil and add the fish and shellfish for a super fast meal for family … or your most important guests.* To make the **<u>single stock recipe</u>** combine the following and simmer 30 minutes:

- *4 tablespoon of organic olive oil*
- *3 large organic garlic cloves*
- *1 bottle of clam juice*
- *1 pound can of whole organic tomatoes broken up*
- *2 cups of organic chicken broth or Imagine No-chicken broth*
- *1 cubed organic unpeeled red potato with the eyes cut out (omit if sensitive to the nightshade family of foods)*
- *1 finely diced large organic carrot*
- *1 finely chopped whole organic celery stalk*
- *several whole sprigs of chopped fresh organic parsley (or dried parsley)*
- *½ teaspoon each of organic dried basil, paprika and thyme (or to taste)*
- *½ teaspoon of natural sea salt (or to taste)*
- *2 bay leaves **removed after cooking***

Taste and adjust seasonings as desired. <u>This stock can now be frozen if 2, 3, or 4 times the recipe is made.</u> **<u>Having fish and chicken stock in your freezer for the base of many quick meals makes you a smart cook . . . and more interesting meals when you are busy!</u>**

To continue with one meal bring desired amount of stock to a boil and add the following (or your choices) to serve 3-4 people:

- *½ package of ecologically raised peeled and deveined medium shrimp*
- *½ pound of clams in the shell **washed very well to get rid of the sand***
- *3 fillets of any ocean fish – <u>for economy you can leave out the shellfish and just use more fish.</u> Optional addition is scallops (cut in half or quarters).*

Cook ocean fish for 10 minutes then add shellfish and cook only 3 more minutes. To determine fish with low mercury check www.realsimple.com/fish. You can use canned tuna, salmon or sardines from Wild Planet that is BPA free and low in mercury.

Serve with any choice of whole grain organic sprouted bread from the health food store. Coat each piece with a mixture of Better Butter and garlic paste you can buy in jars in the health food store. Wrap in foil and heat in the oven until warm. Add a great salad for a **** meal everyone will rave about!

If this is a company dinner, let the meal settle, then serve this simple dessert:

1. Melt ½ cup of Better Butter with ¼ cup organic maple syrup (54 glycemic index) or Coconut Nectar (35 glycemic index). Maple syrup is not as low in glycemic index as Coconut Nectar but is has some important values. Besides having an impressive list of vitamins, minerals and antioxidants, maple syrup causes the genes that produce harmful ammonia in the liver to be less active. Pure 100% maple syrup produced in the U.S. should always be organic. Some trees are kept free flowing with formaldehyde pellets and may be collected in lead buckets, but this practice is outlawed in Canada. All maple syrup coming from Canada is safe.

2. Add 2 mashed **very ripe bananas with brown spots** and cook until soft and blended. *The bananas must be very ripe or the flavor is too mild for the ice cream, and you need to pick another dessert.*

3. Serve under and over any Vanilla non-dairy ice cream layered in crystal stemware. If you have a soy problem the best ice cream is the Bliss brand of Coconut ice cream. Top with finely chopped pecans (or the fabulous pecan sauce recipe on 15) or toasted almonds.

The end of another perfect meal!

CHICKEN OR TURKEY OREGANO

This is a wonderful special event, or company dinner that looks gorgeous to serve makes you look great and you don't have to tell them how easy it was. This is so easy it can also be a family dinner they will appreciate. To serve 2-3 people …

The best chicken parts to use are 4 skinless, boneless thighs in ½ inch slices, or ½ inch slices of 1 **very large** skinless boneless chicken breast, or ½ inch slices of two **small to medium** chicken breasts. You can also use organic turkey thigh or breast meat. If you cannot find turkey parts you can ask the manager of the meat department if he will cut you some turkey parts and you can freeze any extra for a future meal. Sauté the chicken (or turkey) slices *on medium to medium low heat* to prevent burning in the following ingredients. Increase ingredients proportionately to the amount of chicken:

– *¼ cup of organic sesame oil (or you can use olive if it has a mild flavor). Sesame has a taste of its own, so not using it will change the recipe a little. If you double the amount of chicken, ⅓ cup of oil is enough.*

– *One large finely sliced sweet **white or red** organic onion. I prefer to cook with sweet white or red onions because you don't have your dinner ruined if the yellow onion has a strong dominate bite. Even labeled sweet yellow onions will have more of a bite then the sweet white or red onions. White onions are not available during some seasons of the year but organic red onions are usually available. To double the recipe use two large onions or one very large onion.*

– *3 very large thinly sliced organic garlic cloves*

– *½ teaspoon of natural sea salt (or more to taste)*

– *1 high rounded tablespoon of organic dried oregano*

– *Cover with a lid and check often to turn each piece, making sure it is on low simmer and not burning. It takes about 45 minutes to 1 hour. Take 2 tomatoes for each original amount*

155

of chicken in the recipe (using 4 tomatoes if you have 8 thighs, etc.) and cut each tomato in half. This recipe tastes better if the tomatoes are ruby red and delicious. A pink winter tomato just is not the same. Then cut each half in quarters (8 slices per tomato). **When everything else is ready in the meal, and people are seated**, *add the tomatoes to the sauce* **<u>TO HEAT, BUT NOT TO COOK</u>**.

Serve on a platter topped with finely chopped fresh parsley. Add another splash of color with steamed asparagus spears or broccoli. Serve with a whole grain sprouted bread, organic muffin or pop-over; simple mixed salad greens with thin slivers of colorful carrot, croutons and a tasty dressing … or a simple platter of select raw vegetables.

I served this recipe to 6 people with a fan of colorful grilled vegetables around the chicken, and one rosemary potato from the recipe on 28. Aroma can be is a great addition to a company meal so I included whole grain organic sprouted bread sliced in half, stacked and pre-spread with garlic Better Butter and then warmed in foil in the oven.

A simple dessert is **luscious** dairy free organic Natural Choice sorbet with a piece of my no-bake brownie from 13, and a cup of green or herb tea of their choice. Check your health food store for the many flavors of Natural Choice. Dessert can also be any recipe you love that is made healthier with some adjustments. Try to serve dessert one to two hours after dinner and not immediately after the meal for best digestion.

The compliments will be deserved!

DON'T FORGET ABOUT BLACK EYED PEAS

I have a saying, "If it is new and improved, forget it." Generally that applies to modern technology but not in the case of organic canned beans. If you buy dried beans and do not cook them for months or years, they may not cook up soft. If you cook the beans in the recipe instead of precooking and throwing the water out as described in the Nutrition Chapter of my book, you can get gas from the indigestible sugar in the beans. If you buy organic canned beans and **rinse them under running water until all the foam is gone**, they are quick and easy to do whatever you want …**right now!** Add to soups and stews, and look for other ways you can prepare easy to use **organic canned beans that makes the top five meal stretcher suggestions to stretch the budget.**

MY FAVORITE BLACK EYED PEAS RECIPE

*After you have **thoroughly** rinsed all the foam off canned organic black eyes peas add very finely chopped sweet organic **white or red** onions (a lot or a little based on individual taste), and enough organic mayonnaise to taste (I use organic Canola). You may need to add a little sea salt to taste. A great side dish as part of the main meal or the center of a salad. Take for lunch or a party with whole grain crackers.*

MARINATED BLACK EYED PEAS

*After you have **thoroughly** rinsed all the foam off a can of black eyed peas put this recipe together the night before or in the morning to marinate a while. Add the following ingredients or adjust to taste milder or sharper as you prefer:*

- *3 tablespoons of any **mild** tasting organic oil.*
- *1 tablespoon of your favorite vinegar (I use Coconut Secret Vinegar).*
- *½ cup of finely chopped **white or red** organic onions, or use chopped Spring onions. **Do not use strong yellow onions in a raw food recipe.***
- *½ cup of chopped organic parsley or 2 tablespoons organic dried parsley.*
- *1 very large finely chopped organic garlic clove or chopped garlic in a jar.*

- 1 level teaspoon organic dried basil; 1 level teaspoon organic dried oregano.
- ¼ teaspoon of natural sea salt (or more to taste).
- ¼ teaspoon dry mustard (**optional** if you like a sharper bite).
- <u>freshly ground</u> black pepper to taste … **optional** … again adds to the bite

This tastes delicious piled on top of an organic whole grain cracker, add a plate of selective finger food vegetables to munch on, rent a DVD … relax and enjoy! You can also use it as a cold platter side dish for lunch, as part of a salad or a cold side dish to a bland meal like plain broiled fish. This is another good choice for a buffet or party.

Remember: All recipes can **vary** based on where the ingredient is **grown,** personal **taste preference** and **brand** of ingredient used. If you like the idea of a recipe, but it doesn't taste right to you, **<u>adjust the ingredients</u>** and **<u>be creative.</u>**

<u>Cooking is *VERY CREATIVE*</u>. **If you create a successful recipe … beam from ear to ear as you serve it! _I'm always saying, "I found this recipe … but this is Dori's version."_**

BE PROUD OF HOW CREATIVE YOU CAN BE WITH ORGANIC CANNED BEANS.

QUICK BUTTER BEAN SOUP

FROM DORI'S KITCHEN – 21

This Butter Bean Soup uses organic canned beans that *are quick and easy.*

In a large pan with one tablespoon of organic olive oil, sauté the following vegetables for five minutes:

- *Two **very large** red or yellow organic onions chopped small – do not skimp (white onions are too bland for this recipe).*
- *Four **large** organic carrots or ½ bag of organic baby carrots chopped small. Lots of carrots in this recipe adds a special flavor so do not skimp on the carrots.*

Add the following:

- *One quart of organic chicken broth … or No-chicken broth.*
- *One teaspoon of natural sea salt (or more to taste).*
- *Two teaspoons of garlic powder or six large finely chopped organic garlic cloves.*
- *Four cans of organic navy beans that make this recipe easy because they are already cooked. Rinse each can **THOROUGHLY** under running water until **ALL FOAM IS GONE.** This will get rid of the indigestible sugar in beans that cause gas. Some people might get gas from a bean recipe using dried beans, but because canned beans are cooked in liquid, they may have no trouble with this version if they are rinsed properly. **YOU CAN ALSO VARY THIS RECIPE BY CHANGING TO ANOTHER CANNED BEAN OR A VARIETY OF BEANS FOR A VARIATION.***

Slow cook for one hour either on top of the stove, in the oven at 375 degrees or in a slow cooker on low all day. Before serving, add four tablespoons of organic butter (not Better Butter). Butter in this recipe is the secret ingredient, so do not leave it out. Butter is the highest in Vitamins A and D of any food on earth and a little organic butter in moderation is not the bad guy. There is no allergic reaction to butter since it is only the fat and not the allergic properties of protein in milk.

Butter Bean Soup freezes very well, so I usually **double this recipe**. On some busy days you need a break, or you may have unexpected company. Other days, you just want a light meal because you are eating later than you should. You can take this soup from the freezer and put it into a covered casserole in the oven at 350 degrees for one hour to heat while you are making the salad. *How easy is that?*

WAYS TO USE FABULOUS ORGANIC CANNED BEANS:

1. **Toss any bean choice into salads and soups for nutrition and as a budget extender. Always rinse until there is no foam left.**

2. **Puree white beans with garlic, lemon juice and olive oil for an easy dip.**

3. **Combine red beans with buffalo or ostrich hamburger for a taco filling.**

4. **Wrap pinto beans with chopped tomato, chopped lettuce and scallions in a flour tortilla, topped with your favorite salad dressing or a salsa recipe.**

5. **Add cannellini beans into stews for the last 20 minutes of cooking.**

6. **Mix black beans with organic canned corn and add to purchased organic salsa for a great quick side dish.**

<u>Hope you are having a nutritious, delicious day!</u>

CLAM, SALMON, OR CORN FRITTERS

FROM DORI'S KITCHEN – 22

Occasionally you will find a sauce that makes what it covers seem unimportant. This is one of those recipes for family or company meals. *The clam or salmon fritters taste good … but the sauce is fabulous!* ___If you are a vegetarian, make corn fritters.___

Make your sauce first, as the fritters cook up quickly:

1. *Drain the juice off a small can of diced clams, or wild caught canned salmon. Save ¼ cup for the fritters, and put the rest of the juice in a mini- blender bowl. A mini-blender is a must have addition for those small jobs that would get lost in a big blender. It is an inexpensive kitchen tool everyone should have. **If you do not eat clams or salmon, or you are a vegetarian use corn juice from canned corn, or vegetable broth.***

2. *Add a whole small sliced organic cucumber … or spinach if you cannot eat or do not like cucumbers to make the sauce.*

3. *Add one full teaspoon of crushed organic dried rosemary.*

4. *Add 4 tablespoons of organic mayonnaise, or more to make desired thickness.*

5. *Whirl in a blender and save to go over fritters.*

To make the fritters mix together:

- *drained small can of either diced clams … or canned salmon … or organic sweet canned whole corn.*
- *one large organic egg … or 1 tablespoon of sprouted flaxseed to thicken.*
- *¼ cup of the saved liquid … or a little more if too thick with the flaxseed.*
- *¼ cup of any organic whole grain flour like wheat, spelt … or low glycemic index quinoa that is the best digested protein.*
- *1 teaspoon aluminum free baking powder.*
- *¼ teaspoon natural sea salt (or more to taste).*

- 3 tablespoons of finely chopped **white or red** onion (not yellow).
- 1 tablespoon finely chopped organic celery (do not use if celery is bitter).
- 2 tablespoons of melted Better Butter (recipe on 29).
- 2 large finely chopped organic garlic cloves. In this recipe the fresh garlic or chopped garlic in a jar works better than garlic powder.
- 1 tablespoon finely chopped fresh organic parsley (or 1 teaspoon dried).

Spray grill with olive oil spray, and preheat to medium. Drop mixture on grill by tablespoons and brown about 2 minutes on each side. This recipe feeds 2 people, so if you double or triple the recipe keep browned fritters in a warm oven until all are cooked. Serve each fritter (about 6 per person) on a plate with the tasty cucumber or spinach sauce. Some people use warm organic applesauce over fritters but adding fruit to protein and starch is not as good for your digestion.

Serve with one of your award winning salads, or a selection of raw vegetable finger food. Fritters are not ordinary … go ahead and try the unusual.

Our menu is never boring, yet I cook simply and quick! Try new recipes on your day off so you know how easy they are to fix on other busy days.

Enjoy!

HOPE FOR PIZZA AND MACARONI CHEESE LOVERS

You may have just found out you have a dairy allergy, or a wheat allergy, or cannot eat tomatoes or green peppers, and you are sad at the thought of no more pizzas or macaroni and cheese.

HOPE FOR THE PIZZA LOVER: First, I have a client who owns a pizza restaurant and he said it is not unusual for people to order a pizza without cheese. If that is your only problem you can still get pizzas from restaurants. They just give you more sauce and vegetables ... and leave off the hormone and antibiotic processed meats. You can also buy cheese free pizzas in the health food stores and add extra toppings plus tolerated cheeses to bake at home.

The people with a wheat allergy, or sensitivity to the nightshade family and cannot tolerate tomatoes or green peppers have a harder time in a restaurant. *But, there is a lot of hope at home!*

First – *look in a health food store for wheat, spelt, or rice pizza crust you can tolerate.*

Second – *if you cannot tolerate the tomato base, it can be changed to two surprising substitutes you must try before judging because they are both good. One is organic cranberry sauce, and the other is canned sweet potato puree. If these suggestions do not appeal to you just put organic mayonnaise or your favorite mustard over the crust and pile the other ingredients on that. You can also spread the* **hypoallergenic** *Manchego sheep cheese or Water Buffalo mozzarella* **on the crust** *where generally the sauce provides moisture, and add the rest on top of the cheese. Both are available less expensive in wholesale houses like Costco.*

Third – *Add any tolerated food such as:*

- *Artichoke hearts or Palm hearts.*
- *Black or green olives.*
- *Marinated imported small round onions many health food stores carry.*
- *Any shredded (or sliced very fine) organic vegetable of choice that will cook up fast such as green peppers, chopped spinach, or thinly sliced white onions.*

- *Sliced organic tomatoes if tolerated.*
- *Finely chopped organic white or red onions (not yellow), or Spring onions.*
- *whole or minced canned green chiles spread evenly over the top (a nightshade food that may not be tolerated by people with joint symptoms).*
- *Sliced mushrooms if you do not have a severe mold allergy.*
- *You can get a wide variety of processed meats that are now organic and made with healthier animal parts than commercial products. Try crumbled cooked turkey bacon, thin slices of chicken or turkey hot dogs, or organic sausage.*

BEING CREATIVE AND FIXING DELICIOUS FOOD IS FUN! DON'T YOU FEEL GOOD WHEN YOU STRETCH OUT OF YOUR OLD CULINARY MOLD AND TRY SOMETHING NEW? <u>GIVING UP CERTAIN INGREDIENTS DOES NOT HAVE TO BE THE END OF A FAVORITE DISH.</u>

<u>HOPE FOR THE MACARONI CHEESE LOVER:</u>

I had a craving one day for macaroni and cheese that I had not eaten in 30 years. *I decided there had to be a recipe that tasted as good as that crunchy, cheesy top that is on the best you've eaten . . . and still remember. Sooooo ... I experimented one night when my husband was at a meeting. I was so shocked at how good it was that I ate way too much ... and could hardly wait to fix it again. Here is the recipe I proudly pass on to those of you who thought you had your last plate of this "all American recipe." For 2-3 people:*

1. **Boil** *2 cups of Tinkyada brand organic macaroni shaped pasta in* **salted water <u>until almost tender.</u>**

2. **<u>Make a sauce</u>** *of 2 cups rice milk or coconut milk mixed with 3 tablespoons Quinoa flour until smooth, 1 tablespoon butter, 2 teaspoons of your favorite mustard, ½ teaspoon garlic powder, ½ teaspoon dried minced onion, ½ teaspoon natural sea salt, 1 tablespoon dried parsley.*

3. **Spray** *a casserole and poor sauce over cooked macaroni.*

4. **Sprinkle top** *generously with gluten free all purpose crumbs. The brand I used was ORGRAN that I use for lots of recipes like coating baked fish, chicken or vegetables ... or used as a filler, thickener or crumb base.*

5. **Top** *crumbs generously with Better Butter pats.*

6. **Top** *Better Butter generously and completely with slices or grated Manchego sheep cheese. The thickness of the cheese depends on how much cheese taste you like. The taste will also vary based on the age of the cheese. Older aged cheese is stronger than the 6 month cheese.*

One year old aged cheese is very strong. Manchego cheese is very expensive, and the 6 month aged cheese is available reasonably priced at Costco and other discount locations.

7. **Bake** *at 350 degrees for 1 hour or until top gets a nice crusty brown.*

Make yourself a perfect salad, and get ready to remember the good old days.

REMEMBER TO ADJUST YOUR FAVORITE RECIPES INSTEAD OF THROWING THEM OUT IF YOU NEED DIETARY CHANGES.

QUESADILLAS

I cannot encourage you enough to buy a Quesadilla Maker. It can make quick meals, company meals … *and always fun meals.* If you have kitchen helpers and are making multiple Quesadillas, you can get an assembly line going that is fun for everyone. For every finished Quesadilla that feeds one adult or two children, you need two whole wheat, whole Spelt, or rice tortillas. For four people, line eight tortillas across a counter. The following are all the 'fun' additions you place on the tortillas until **you 'build' what you want it to be.** <u>*Consider using your choice of the following as* **moisture free** *as possible because* **a soggy Quesadilla will not release well from the pan:**</u>

1. *Spread a THIN LAYER of organic mayonnaise on BOTH tortillas to the edge.*

2. *Spread a THIN LAYER of your favorite mustard on BOTH tortillas to the edge.*

3. *Wash hands well and* **<u>squeeze all the liquid</u>** *out of a handful of organic relish, and spread on ONE tortilla to the edge; or use a thick salsa spread thin.*

4. *Slice organic* **white or red** *onions only (not yellow onions) into* <u>*tissue thin slices,*</u> *and spread over ONE tortilla to the edge.*

5. *Slice (do not chop or extra moisture will soften tortillas and make it hard to get out of the Quesadilla Maker) organic tomatoes and spread evenly over ONE tortilla.*

6. *Take a paper towel and* **blot liquid off** *canned* **whole** *mild, roasted and peeled green chiles cut into strips and spread evenly over ONE tortilla. If you cannot find Natural Value canned whole green chiles, check* www.NaturalValue.com. **<u>Squeeze off the liquid</u>** *if you use canned* **diced** *green chiles.*

7. **At this point you can put a choice of protein selections over ONE tortilla:**

   – *Applegate Farms organic roasted or smoked turkey or ham slices. If you cannot find it call 1-800-587-5858, or check* www.applegatefarms.com.

- Cooked and crumbled ostrich sausage patties – tastes great!
- Cooked and crumbled turkey bacon – another good choice!
- Cooked and crumbled buffalo or ostrich ground meat that is salted as desired.
- **Drained** canned shrimp, or frozen cooked, and peeled shrimp thawed and **blotted dry.** Thawed cooked frozen shrimp tastes better than canned.
- **Drained** canned and crumbled sardines or tuna … or anchovies that come in a jar. Any choice you want! **BE CREATIVE!**

8. Shred Manchego sheep cheese and put over ONE tortilla, **but not close to the edge** so it does not melt out when cooked. **Do not use any cheese if you have a serious mold reaction as all cheese will have some mold.**

9. **When assembled,** put second tortilla over the top; put into the **sprayed** Quesadilla Maker that has been preheated. Many times the lid does not close well because of all the filling, so I take a kitchen towel and hold the top down with pressure. It takes five minutes to lightly brown the tortillas, but you can open and check for doneness.

NOTE: After you finish cooking, wipe excess cheese off right away and put a damp cloth over grill as you close lid. This keeps it moist for easy cleaning later.

10. **Serve with a platter of raw vegetable selections, and enjoy the happy energy around the table!**

EVERYONE LOVES TO EAT FUN FOOD, AND WHEN IT IS ALSO HEALTHY AND NUTRITIOUS YOU HAVE A WINNER!

CHICKEN PAPRIKA

This has been a favorite family recipe for 50 years, requested at special occasions like birthdays, etc. It is a version of an original Polish recipe that used sour cream, and was called Chicken Paprikosh. I lost touch with it when I got away from allergic dairy products. *One day I was fooling around with ingredients and found that using organic Canola mayonnaise or Old Chatham sheep yogurt mimicked sour cream to the point that the recipe tasted minimally different.* **Here is the 'old' recipe that feeds 2-3 people with a 'new twist' that makes it healthier:**

1. *Cook a finely chopped **white or red** onion (not yellow onion) or 2 inches of a leek with ...*

   - *3 tablespoons of Better Butter (recipe on 29).*
   - *3 tablespoons of paprika.*
   - *4 tablespoons of Coconut vinegar.*
   - *3 tablespoons of Coconut Nectar.*
   - *1 cup of organic chicken stock or No-chicken broth.*
   - *1 teaspoon of natural sea salt ... add more later to taste.*
   - *6 pieces of skinless chicken legs, or skinless thighs, or skinless and boneless thighs. You can also use breast meat if that is what you prefer, and cut up into 1-2 inch squares. Bring to a slow simmer and cook **covered** for 20 minutes, making sure it does not burn.*

2. *Thicken with another cup of chicken stock mixed with 3 mounded tablespoons of any whole grain flour (I use Quinoa), and slowly stir into pan. Cook on simmer for another 20-30 minutes with the lid on and watch to make sure is does not burn. The amount of thickening varies on how much liquid boiled away and size of the chicken pieces that adds juice. You may need to add another tablespoon of flour.*

3. *While chicken is simmering, cook 2 cups of organic whole grain macaroni in salted water. I use organic Spelt or Tinkyada Rice pasta that I think has better texture and taste than whole wheat.*

4. *When chicken is tender mix ½ cup broth with either 1 cup of sheep yogurt (not goat*

yogurt) or 6 tablespoons of Canola mayonnaise and add to skillet to blend but do not boil. REMEMBER SHEEP YOGURT AND ALSO CANOLA MAYO MIMICS SOUR CREAM FOR A SIMILAR TASTE WITHOUT THE COW DAIRY.

5. *Stir in cooked and drained tolerated macaroni; add more salt to taste.*

This recipe is a wonderful family special dinner or company dinner, **but it needs color.** *Serve with one of your prize winning salads, a plate of grilled vegetables from the recipe on 7, or a colorful cooked vegetable.* **You WILL get compliments!**

WANT A QUICK CRUNCHY OVEN BAKED CHICKEN RECIPE?

Melt 4 tbsp. Better Butter and coat 2 chicken breasts that are each cut into 3 strips. Coat chicken strips with a mixture of tolerated bread crumbs or rice crumbs, 1 tbsp. parsley flakes, 1 tsp. garlic powder, 1 tbsp. onion flakes, and ½ tsp. sea salt. Optional coating is to add 1 tbsp. olive oil to your favorite mustard choice and then coat with crumbs. Bake at 400 degrees for about 30 minutes.

Compliments again!

CHICKEN OR TURKEY PILAF

Hormone and antibiotic free chicken or turkey is clearly a protein staple. Turkey is not just for the holidays. There are so many recipes you can use chicken and turkey in everyday and company meals. This recipe feeds 2-3 people …

1. *In a skillet with a lid sauté 2 tablespoons of organic olive oil with ⅓ cup of 1 inch pieces of a thin organic uncooked tolerated pasta* **until golden brown.**

2. *Add one* **large** *white, red, or yellow onion sliced. Many of the recipes that call for a delicate flavor are best made with sweet and mild white or red onions. Stir-fries, oven baked dishes and recipes with sauces are examples of recipes that may tolerate a sharper yellow onion.*

3. *Add 3 very* **large** *finely chopped organic garlic cloves. I use garlic in a lot of recipes and when I have time I prefer to chop up the garlic cloves. The next best thing to fresh garlic is garlic paste or organic Emperor's Kitchen chopped garlic (use up in one month). But any recipe will come out close if you use the organic garlic powder. I usually add ½ teaspoon of garlic powder for each very large fresh garlic clove used in the recipe. You may want to adjust that differently. LEARN TO BE A PERSONAL COOK AND ADJUST YOUR RECIPES TO TASTE JUST RIGHT FOR YOU.* **RECIPES SHOULD BE IDEAS … NOT THE LAST WORD. LEARN TO MAKE A NEW MEAL CONCEPT YOUR ORIGINAL!**

   - *1 tablespoon of organic dried parsley or 2 tablespoons of fresh parsley.*
   - *¾ cup of any whole grain brown rice or any of the combination rice mixes that are in health food stores. Look for whole grain … and organic!*

4. *Add 4 raw, skinless and boneless cubed chicken thighs … or 2 cubed chicken breasts … or 1 cubed small turkey breast.*

5. *Add 2 cups of organic chicken stock. I always keep 2 boxes of organic chicken broth in the pantry to have on hand for many last minute meal recipes.* **This is one stock item you**

never want to be without. I prefer the Imagine brand of Organic Free Range Chicken Broth that is fat free, gluten free, and no MSG. **If you are vegetarian you can get Imagine brand No-chicken broth to use in recipes.**

6. Add ½ teaspoon **each** of organic dried oregano, crushed rosemary, marjoram and basil. You can adjust herbs to taste, or use fresh herbs if available.

7. Add 1 teaspoon of natural sea salt … more or less to taste.

8. Bring to a boil, then simmer **COVERED** on low heat for 60 minutes until rice is soft. Do not lift the lid for 30 minutes. Then check to make sure you still have liquid, and if you need more liquid add a little extra chicken broth. You can also cook this in a 375 degree oven for 1 ½ hours until the rice is tender.

9. Serve portions topped with **optional** freshly ground organic black pepper, and **definitely** slivered organic almonds if tolerated for that gourmet touch.

This recipe is delicious, but needs color on the plate. You can serve it with a beautiful salad, or raw vegetable 'finger food', or a cooked vegetable choice, or grilled vegetables.

**CONGRATUATIONS
ANOTHER EASY WINNING DINNER!**

MEAT OR VEGETARIAN HASH

Hash recipes are very easy to prepare. Lamb is easier to digest than beef or pork and has minimal if any hormones and antibiotics added so it is the best red meat to order in a restaurant. All red meat recipes are better digested if your saliva pH is 6.6 -7.0. Hash recipes can be very delicious and can be changed in so many ways by using lamb, chicken, turkey, buffalo, ostrich or make it vegetarian with beans. I'll acquaint you with a few variations in this recipe but first here is the basic beginning to any hash combination:

- *Brown 1 pound of your choice of organic ground meat in a skillet that has a lid with a little olive oil, and drain off the fat. For extra draining of any fat put the ground meat on multiple paper towels, blot out excess fat and return to the skillet.* **If you are not using meat add the beans later.** *Now sauté with the meat or with a little olive oil …*
- *1 large chopped organic red or yellow onion.*
- *6 <u>large</u> fresh garlic cloves … or garlic paste … or chopped garlic.*
- *1 tablespoon of organic dried parsley or 2 tablespoons of organic fresh parsley.*
- *1 teaspoon of natural sea salt or more to taste.*
- *½ teaspoon each of the following organic herbs: crumbled rosemary, basil, oregano, thyme and sage.*

This is your base recipe … **be creative and add <u>'one'</u> of the following:**

- *A traditional hash recipe calls for potatoes. Cut up 2 organic unpeeled* **red** *potatoes with the eyes cut out into small cubes, add 1 cup of chicken broth and cook in mixture until soft. Anytime the mixture gets too dry just add more chicken broth. Organic red potatoes are easier to digest than white potatoes.*

- **Or** *…Cook 1 cup of any organic macaroni shape in salted water. Drain, rinse and add to the skillet along with 1 cup of organic chicken broth. You can add a little more macaroni if you want to stretch the meal. I use spelt or Tinkyada rice macaroni.*

- **Or** *…Continue cooking in skillet after adding ¾ cup of any organic brown rice like Jasmine or Basmati, or any organic rice blend with 2 cups of chicken broth. Try to find the*

Lundberg Quick Wild Rice that cooks in 30 minutes and opens up like popcorn. Cover and cook until rice is soft, adding more chicken broth if needed.

— *Or ... add thoroughly rinsed canned organic beans instead of meat.*

— *Optional addition to any hash recipe is sliced yellow and green zucchini, or chopped organic green pepper. **ALWAYS** taste raw zucchini first to make sure it is not bitter, and could ruin your recipe.*

— *You can completely change the taste of the recipe by adding 2 or more tablespoons of organic Canola mayonnaise or sheep yogurt (not goat).*

<u>Hash recipes are inexpensive and tasty</u>, but they have little color to excite your interest so serve with colorful vegetables.

Many recipes just give you an idea, and you can use your CREATIVE ABILITY to make it YOUR RECIPE!

BAKED FISH AND ROSEMARY POTATOES

*People who do not like fish may **not** have tasted well prepared fish often enough to realize preparation can make **ALL THE DIFFERENCE!** I agree that fish not purchased fresh, dry and overcooked is not a treat.* <u>MOST PEOPLE OVERCOOK FISH!</u> *Please read the whole 'Fish' section in the Nutrition Chapter of my book for easy, great tasting ideas. **This combination helps you learn to use your time in the kitchen wisely.***

FIRST START THE CRISPY ROASTED POTATOES WITH ROSEMARY

1. *Buy 6 organic small round red potatoes and cut out any eyes. Scrub well but do not peel and cut in half or quarters based on size. Always cut the eyes out of **any potato** as there is a toxic element to the eye that is best not eaten. **If you cannot eat red potatoes the same recipe works with peeled cubed sweet potatoes.***

2. *Put prepared potatoes in a medium skillet on medium heat with 1 tablespoons of organic olive oil. Turn frequently to lightly brown on all sides for 10 minutes.*

3. *Add 1 teaspoon of organic dried whole rosemary (crushed) and stir into potatoes.*

4. *Melt 2 tablespoons Better Butter with ½ teaspoon sea salt, and coat potatoes.*

5. *Move to a sprayed uncovered casserole dish and bake 45 minutes at 375 degrees.*

6. *Lower the heat to 350 degrees and place the casserole of fish fillets below in the oven with the potatoes. Continue with the cooking time for the fish.*

BAKED FISH OF CHOICE

1. *Oil or spray a casserole dish large enough to handle very lightly salted BONELESS fish fillets (½ lb. per person) in a single layer. Try any mild tasting fish like sole, haddock, scrod (that is baby cod and tastes much milder than the larger cod), flounder, Orange Roughy,*

ocean (or ecologically farm raised) Tilapia. Check the Internet www.realsimple.com/ fishguide for the fish lowest in mercury.

2. *Make a mixture of ½ cup of organic Canola mayonnaise and 1 tablespoon of your favorite mustard. You may need to make more depending on the number of fillets. Spread mixture over fillets evenly.*

3. *Bake at 350 degrees for 15-20 minutes depending on the thickness of the fish.*

HERE IS WHERE THE TRICK IS … DO NOT OVERCOOK!

These fish fillets and roasted potatoes look great with bright vegetables like cherry tomatoes or asparagus. With organization this combination works well together. By the time the fish and potatoes are done, the kitchen can be clean, the table is set and **YOU LOOK RELAXED AND READY TO ENJOY DINNER … DON'T FORGET AFTER THE COMPLIMENTS TO SMILE AND SAY … IT WAS EASY!**

CLAM STUFFED MUSHROOMS

For company appetizer: CLAM STUFFED MUSHROOMS (shrimp, or tuna): *Remove stems from 1 ½ lb.* **medium same size** *mushrooms and chop stems. Cook* **stems** *with 1 large minced garlic clove in ¼ cup butter until liquid is gone. Drain 2 (6 oz.) cans chopped clams* **saving** *2 tbsp. liquid. To cooked stems add clams, clam liquid, 1 cup of tolerated breadcrumbs, ¼ cup fresh parsley and ½ tsp. sea salt. Brush inside mushrooms with melted butter and fill with mixture; place on greased baking sheet, and broil 10 minutes or until brown.*

YOU WILL HAVE VERY HAPPY GUESTS!

ROSEMARY CHICKEN

FROM DORI'S KITCHEN – 29

This is the meal for you to make if you want a dinner that makes the house smell DELICIOUS while it is cooking. *It is a good dinner to fix if you need to get dinner started and do something else for an hour. Put together this easy oven recipe:*

1. *Spray a shallow baking pan that has a lid.*

2. *Skin 4 **large** hormone and antibiotic free chicken thighs, or buy skinless and boneless thighs, or 4-6 skinned chicken legs, or 2 large chicken breasts if you prefer white meat. Lay chicken single file in the casserole.*

3. *Cut a **medium** white, red, or yellow onion into slices, or use ½ **of a large onion**. Lay onion slices over the chicken.*

4. *In a saucepan heat the following ingredients together:*

    *   *1 cup of organic catsup*
    *   *3 tablespoons of Coconut Vinegar or Balsamic Vinegar*
    *   *4 tablespoons Better Butter you made (recipe below)*
    *   *2 large minced garlic, or garlic paste, or Emperor's chopped garlic*
    *   *1 teaspoon of finely crushed organic dried rosemary*
    *   *½ teaspoon of organic dried basil and ½ teaspoon natural sea salt*

5. *Pour sauce over the onions in the casserole, cover and bake at 350 degrees for 1 hour and 15 minutes. If you did other things while the chicken was cooking, go back into the kitchen after 1 hour.*

6. *Cook 6 ounces of tolerated whole grain noodles in salted water until tender.*

7. *The chicken has now been in the oven for an extra 15 minutes. Remove chicken from the casserole, and stir the drained and rinsed noodles into the sauce. **The smell will drive you wild!***

8. *Place the chicken pieces on the serving plates, and the beautiful red noodles around the edge of the chicken. Consider grilling yellow or green zucchini cut in half lengthwise with Better Butter that is high in Vitamin A and Vitamin D. These long grilled vegetables look beautiful surrounding any main course.*

BETTER BUTTER

The **Better Butter recipe** can easily be made in a food processor, or in a **deep** mixing bowl if the butter is **very soft**. *Take a pound of organic butter, 1 cup of any mild tasting organic oil (not strong tasting olive oil) and 1 cup of filtered water added slowly. Mix to a satin smooth and store in a covered container in the refrigerator. This **easy to spread** butter is now ready for the next time you need butter. Do not use **Better Butter** in any baking recipe that calls for **butter** as the liquid addition may change the outcome of the recipe.* If you are a single person, freeze 2 cubes of butter and make ½ of the recipe at a time.

A delicious salad helps stretch the meal to feed 4 people. *On organic salad greens, add your favorite vinaigrette recipe, sprinkle with organic dried cranberries and pumpkinseeds; top with **thin** slices of Manchego sheep cheese . . . **beautiful!***

THIS MEAL WILL HAVE DINNER PARTICIPANTS APPRECIATE YOUR CULINARY TALENT!

A SIMPLE MEAT OR VEGETARIAN CASSEROLE

FROM DORI'S KITCHEN – 30

Some days you feel creative, and some days you don't. **Today I felt creative**, and wondered what to do with the lamb shoulder chops I got from the freezer. *I decided to add a little of this and that and see what happened.* **This recipe turned out GREAT ... with the added benefit of feeling really good about myself.**

My recipes usually start with an idea from a book or magazine. I change some ingredients to be healthier, *so in some degree ... all my recipes are original.* You could also use chicken, turkey, buffalo or ostrich; or **adjust for a vegetarian casserole.** *Here is what I did in my stainless steel slow cooker (also known as a crock pot):*

1. *Take the fat off the edge of lamb shoulder chops you need for your dinner (I had 2 chops, but the rest of the recipe was enough for 3 people). Lamb shoulder chops are the best cut because they cook up tender in any oven or slow cooker recipe but are not expensive like the higher priced cuts. Australian lamb from Costco is less expensive. Lamb has the least hormones and antibiotics of any red meat because they are young, and the best red meat to order in a restaurant.*

2. *Simmer trimmed chops on medium heat in 2 tablespoons of organic olive oil and add:*

    – *½ teaspoon each of organic dried basil, oregano, marjoram and thyme. Organic dried herbs are what most people use in any recipe. Fresh herbs are great if you grow them, or can quickly use the amount you purchase easily before they spoil.*
    – *1 sliced <u>medium or ½ large</u> white, red, or yellow organic onion.*
    – *1 teaspoon of natural sea salt adjusted to taste.*
    – *1 tablespoon of organic dried parsley or 2 tablespoons of fresh parsley. Fresh parsley can be put in nearly every recipe you make because it is good for digestion. My dried parsley is a back up when I am out of fresh parsley.*
    – *1 teaspoon of organic garlic powder or 2 large diced garlic cloves. My garlic powder is a back up when I am out of fresh garlic and I usually use powdered garlic in casseroles, hashes, stews, etc. because the garlic flavor is part of a whole recipe. Use fresh garlic for a delicate flavor or if the texture of diced fresh garlic helps the recipe.*

- *1 medium 14 ½ ounce can of organic diced tomatoes with garlic and onion (or plain organic canned diced or whole tomatoes if you cannot find it). If you cannot tolerate tomatoes be really creative and try a can of organic sweet potatoes.*
- *1 cup of brown rice. I always use organic gluten free Lundberg Brown Basmati or Jasmine rice because of the aromatic qualities and more flavorful than traditional brown rice. If you cannot find them check www.lundberg.com.*
- *2 ½ cups of organic chicken (or vegetable) broth (or more if needed during cooking).*

3. ***Slow** cook for 2 hours, or until rice is soft; check occasionally to stir.*

4. *Take all meat off the bone and stir into the rice; **vegetarians add Quinoa seeds for part of the rice that gives you a complete protein.***

5. *Just before serving add 3 tablespoons of organic Canola mayonnaise or sheep yogurt (not goat) to make the rice mixture creamy and delicious.*

6. *Serve with a fabulous salad, or vegetable finger food.*

My husband's smile and compliment was enough for me to sit down at the computer after dinner to write down the recipe WITH PRIDE!

GREAT SAUCES OVER DROP BISCUITS

This versatile recipe is a good one because it is **SOOOOOO quick and easy to fix and is easy to adjust to vegetarian diets.** *Some days you are rushed or forget to get something out of the freezer, or have left over protein to figure out how to use. If you have more time in the morning than at dinner, fix the crème sauce and put in the refrigerator to bring out and heat at dinner. While the simple drop biscuits are baking for 10-15 minutes, you can make a salad, and dinner is ready SO QUICK!*

The **drop biscuits** *are easy to make in a preheated 350 degree oven:*

1. Combine the following in a medium bowl for 2-3 people ...

    - *1 cup of organic whole spelt or Quinoa flour.*
    - *½ tablespoon of any mild tasting organic oil.*
    - *½ tablespoon of aluminum free baking powder.*
    - *½ cup of any non-dairy milk.*
    - *½ teaspoon of natural sea salt.*

2. *Mix with a fork until blended. Spoon evenly on a sprayed cookie sheet to make 6 biscuits ... then* **lightly** *flatten just to even out the top.*

3. *Bake 12-15 minutes.*

The sauce *is easy to make:*

1. *Put 4 tablespoons of Better Butter (recipe on 29) into a medium skillet and sauté 1 medium or ½ large organic* **white or red** *onion for 5 minutes.*

2. *Add ½ teaspoon of natural sea salt adjusted to taste.*

3. *Add 1 tablespoon of organic dried parsley or 2 tablespoons of fresh parsley.*

4. *Add either 2 large chopped organic garlic … or 1 teaspoon of garlic powder … or 2 teaspoons of chopped garlic in a jar.*

5. *Add ½ cup of any non-dairy milk like original organic rice milk or almond milk, mixed with 1 tablespoons of organic Quinoa flour . . . or double this for more sauce.*

6. *Add 1 tablespoon of organic Canola mayonnaise or sheep (not goat) adding a touch of spark to the sauce.*

7. **Cut up and add the protein of choice to the sauce:** *Cooked chicken or turkey meat, left over sausage or bacon, a can of Wild Planet tuna or salmon including the juice, cooked shrimp or lump crabmeat, chopped hard boiled eggs with some Manchego cheese added to melt.*

Make it vegetarian with any protein of choice like organic canned beans rinsed until all foam is gone, 2-3 tbsp. Quinoa flakes (a complete protein) and 1 scoop of sprouted flaxseed.

Serve over the baked biscuits with a salad, or vegetable finger food. My husband considers himself a 'lab rat' and is so funny with a new recipe. He holds his fork but does not take a bite until he watches the expression on my face after I take a bite. *I always ask my husband to rate a new recipe and he gave this recipe using left over chicken on a scale of 1-10, a 9, which is a great rating for a dinner that only took me 30 minutes in the kitchen.*

ONLY 30 MINUTES TO MAKE A UNIQUE HEALTHY MEAL IS A 10 FOR ME!

SIDE DISH VEGETABLES

Some meals balance better with a starch or cooked vegetables. I want to remind you that a purist may find fault with some of my meal combining. **If you are sick, complex combinations that require more digestion are not a good idea.** However, we are a society that loves 'recipes.' **TO HANDLE A MORE COMPLEX DIET YOU SHOULD DRINK ½ -1 GLASS OF WATER BEFORE EACH MEAL, HAVE A SALIVA pH OF 6.6 – 7.0, EAT SLOWLY, CHEW YOUR FOOD WELL, BE PLEASANT AT MEALTIME, KEEP FRUIT AND SUGAR AWAY FROM THE MAIN MEAL, AND LIVE BY THE LAWS OF WELLNESS. YOU SHOULD BE ABLE TO ENJOY ORGANIC RECIPES THAT ARE FIXED WITH WHOLE FOODS, SERVED WITH COLOR ... AND ENJOYED!!!** *Here are two more 'special effects' for your meal:*

GREEK OVEN FRIES

1. <u>*Scrub*</u> *4-6 organic* **red** *potatoes (easier to digest than white potatoes) and cut out any eyes ... or peel 2 sweet potatoes. Cut each lengthwise into 8 wedges and place in a covered dish with cold water for 30 minutes. Drain and pat dry.*

2. *Toss potatoes with 2 teaspoons of olive oil, 1 teaspoon of organic dried oregano, and ½ teaspoon natural sea salt.*

3. *Place skin side down on a sprayed baking sheet.*

4. *Bake at 400 degrees until tender and browned. Depending on your oven this takes from 45 to 50 minutes or more.*

5. *Remove from the oven, and sprinkle with organic vinegar (Malt vinegars can contain MSG so always use organic Balsamic or Coconut Secret Vinegar).*

6. *Serve baked fries immediately to add interest to a plain main course.* ***ENJOY!***

MASHED CAULIFLOWER

If you do not like cauliflower … **please try this delicious recipe.** If you like cauliflower and cannot eat potatoes this makes a great substitute for mashed potatoes!

1. *Clean separated flowers of the cauliflower and put into water just to cover. Cook until tender and drink the delicious, nutritious mineral water.*

2. *Place cooked cauliflower into a mixing bowl and with an electric mixer and whip into a soft mashed consistency.*

3. *Add any non-dairy milk, Better Butter (recipe on 29), and natural sea salt to taste (these ingredients vary based on the amount of cauliflower used).*

4. *Optional addition is a little organic mayonnaise that mimics sour cream.*

5. *Serve whipped cauliflower plain or top with crumbled organic turkey bacon, a mix of sunflower and pumpkin or pine nuts that you should have in your freezer. You can also top with shredded Manchego sheep cheese.*

6. *For a gourmet version, you can fold the crumbled bacon into the mixture and put into a sprayed casserole with the shredded cheese on top. Bake at 350 degrees for 20 minutes or until the cheese melts.*

DELICATA SQUASH

You may think that if you eat squash you have to peel, cut it up, bake for about an hour and too often for this nutritious food you give up on the idea. THAT IS NOT THE CASE WITH DELICATA SQUASH! Delicata squash is a small oblong squash, striped yellow and green that has skin so tender you can eat the skin as you quickly stir-fry a recipe. The skin is barely detectable when cooked. I've seen delicate squash bigger than a russet potato and I have not tried that size for skin tenderness. Once you have it you will look for it every fall. To fix …

1. *Cut the squash in half and scoop out the seeds.*

2. *Then slice each half in **very** thin slices across the width.*

3. *Stir-fry or steam until tender for about 20 minutes if you slice thin enough. The stir-fry recipe varies only with your imagination … onions, herbs, toasted nuts, added to your choice of meat … or roast in the oven with olive oil, sea salt onion slices or cinnamon. Try all combinations with this incredible easy to fix squash and I'm sure you will have more than one favorite recipe.*

BRUSSELS SPROUTS

This vegetable unfortunately gets a bad rap. It can be delicious with the right recipe. Try these **OPTIONS** after you boil them in salted water until tender:

1. *Sauté in olive oil with sliced onions and lemon juice. Top with toasted pecans or toasted sesame seeds.*

2. *Sauté in dark sesame oil, chopped onions, minced ginger and minced garlic. Top with chopped Spring onions or chopped leeks and Coconut Secret Aminos.*

3. *Sauté in olive oil, chopped onions and garlic; top with shredded Manchego sheep cheese.*

4. *Cook 3 slices of organic turkey bacon and chop fine. Sauté cooked Brussels Sprouts with ¼ teaspoon dried thyme and lots of chopped onions based on taste in a little chicken or No-chicken broth. Top with chopped bacon.*

5. *Another version of fixing Brussels Sprouts is to not pre-boil, but sauté until tender in 2 tablespoons of water and olive oil. Continue to cook until tender and browned as the sprouts start to caramelize, then drizzle with lemon juice.*

GREEN BEANS

Long, trimmed on the ends but uncut green beans are a summer favorite but too often are just cooked with a little butter or snapped into small pieces. Frozen green beans tend to be snapped. Try these recipes after you just end trim green beans and cook until tender in salted water for a new appearance to your meal and a taste treat change:

1. *Slice at least 4 large garlic cloves and toast in a little butter and olive oil until slightly brown. Stir in cooked green beans and enjoy!*

2. *In 1 tablespoon dark sesame oil sauté minced garlic cloves, sea salt to taste and 1 tablespoon Coconut Aminos. Stir in cooked green beans and top with toasted sesame seeds.*

3. *Cook 3 slices of turkey bacon and remove from pan. Chop into small pieces and set aside. In the pan sauté about 4 Spring onions for a mild onion flavor and add sea salt to taste. Stir in cooked green beans and top with bacon …*

enjoy!

OTHER VEGETABLES TOO MANY PEOPLE IGNORE

1. *Napa cabbage (milder than cabbage) is delicious as an addition to raw salads or cooked stir-fried.*

2. *Kale or Swiss Chard can be cut up in small pieces with the largest part of the stock avoided and cooked in a little water until tender. Seasoning is easy with toasted sesame seeds, butter and sea salt. Chopped cooked turkey bacon is great on kale.*

3. *Do not wait to go to a Chinese restaurant to get snow peas. They are great as an addition to any stir-fry or salad.*

4. *Bamboo shoots add great crunch and a filler to stretch stir-fries.*

5. *Eggplant can be peeled and sliced, then coated with your favorite seasoned and tolerated bread crumbs, then baked for 30 minutes in a 350 degree oven. Experiment with the bread crumb seasoning to include any of the following: chopped onion, chopped green pepper, garlic, herbs of choice and shredded Manchego sheep cheese.*

6. *Leeks can be used in any recipe that calls for onions and has a milder flavor. The green part of leeks can be added to flavor soups, stews and stir-fries ... besides cooked recipes the white part can also be chopped and added to any raw recipe. Leeks may be easier to digest for some people than stronger onions.*

These are just a few of the vegetables you may not be eating. <u>When you shop for vegetables next time and see one you have never tried, ask a clerk to tell you about it ... and some cooking ideas.</u> They may have a simple suggestion that will give you a new taste treat.

Most people are in a cooking rut ... too busy or uninformed to break out of a well worn mold. You, however, are now a creative cook so go for it and try something new. I can't, I don't like, I don't want to and any other negative "stinking thinking" that keeps you in a rut and robs you of new experiences should by now be a part of your past ... not your progressive and experiential future. Life if full of surprises ... and many can be pleasant surprises because <u>you allowed yourself to experience something new.</u>

Enjoy all the above winners!

THE FORGOTTEN VEGETABLES

Many people think they have had their vegetable for the day if they have a salad with lettuce, tomato and cucumber. Too few people eat the full spectrum of the vegetable kingdom. Many fussy eaters from childhood grow up to be fussy adult eaters, limiting their diet to a shockingly short list of foods. Here are a few suggestions for vegetables everyone should be **as** familiar with as the standard list of vegetables. I've already included some recipes for vegetables you may want to try, and here are a few more …

SPINACH is too often eaten raw in salads when it should be eaten steamed due to phytates that if eaten raw all the time can reduce the absorbability of the nutrients in that food. Spinach can taste delicious if seasoned with Coconut Vinegar or lemon juice and sweetened with Coconut Crystals to taste with a dash of sea salt. Masking spinach in a recipe like this one can fool even the fussiest eater, or **impress company** …

1. *Cook 4 slices of organic turkey bacon in a skillet and then cut into small pieces.*
2. *Pat 3 scallops per person with paper towels and sprinkle with natural sea salt. Add to the bacon pan and cook 2 ½ minutes on each side or until done, and transfer to a plate to keep warm in the oven.* **<u>You can use shrimp or any fish you prefer to make this dish.</u>**
3. *Add 1 cup of chopped onion and 6 large sliced garlic cloves (or look for jars of chopped garlic) to the pan and sauté about 3-4 minutes.*
4. *Add 12 ounces of fresh baby spinach to the pan and sauté until wilted. If you cannot get fresh spinach you can buy frozen organic spinach. Season to taste with natural sea salt and optional freshly ground black pepper.*
5. *Divide spinach onto 4 plates and top with crumbled bacon and scallops.*
6. *Drizzle very lightly with fresh lemon juice and serve immediately.*

PARSNIPS are forgotten by the average cook, but when peeled and cut into pieces will add a potato like addition to soups and stews; and can be eaten raw. They look like a fat white carrot, and are often in dishes that contain carrots. Small parsnips are sweeter and generally will be tender … unlike large parsnips that can have a woody core.

Try these recipes:

- Peel, slice and sauté in a little olive oil and water, lemon juice and sea salt.
- Peel, slice and roast in a 400 degree oven for 30-45 minutes seasoned with sea salt and nutmeg.

JICAMA (pronounced Hi-Ku-Muh) is delicious cooked or eaten raw once the woody peel is cut off. It is as easy to peel as a potato. Cut into shoestrings, Jicama looks and tastes like potatoes. Cooked or raw Jicama is a unique and delicious substitute for potatoes in any recipe. Jicama has a mild sweet crunch and is like biting into sugar cane, yet it is low in calories, high in fiber and Vitamin C. If you want a delicious raw diet food to crunch on … think of Jicama.

Try these recipes …

- *Stir raw shoestring cut Jicama in 2 tablespoon sesame oil, 2 crushed garlic cloves, 3 tablespoons chopped red bell pepper (optional), ⅛ teaspoon paprika, and ⅛ teaspoon or more to taste of natural sea salt for about 10 minutes. Top with freshly ground black pepper (optional).*

- *Bake shoestring cut Jicama in a 350 degree oven with a variety of seasonings like: sea salt and olive oil; sea salt and Coconut Vinegar; sea salt and Coconut Aminos.*

KOHLRABI (pronounced Kol-ROB-ee) resembles a turnip only is sweeter and more delicate in flavor. The bulb part is usually light green but can be purple, and the green leaves can be cooked like any greens. The name means cabbage-turnip in German and tastes a lot like the stock part of broccoli.

Try these recipes:

- Cut into slivers it adds crunch to a salad. Look for small ones if you are going to eat it raw.
- Cooked in salted water for 15 minutes can be seasoned as desired for a side dish.
- Roast in a 450 degree oven for 30-35 minutes and sprinkle with sea salt and Coconut Vinegar.

TURNIPS can be a delicious substitute for potatoes. Large turnips can be strong tasting and woody so I prefer the small white turnips that do not need to be peeled and are sweet and mild. If white turnips are not available get the **smallest** purplish turnips that do not have to be peeled. Turnips can be eaten raw, boiled, sautéed or roasted.

CHICKEN WITH DUMPLINGS OR NOODLES

FROM DORI'S KITCHEN – 34

This **old time favorite** is easier to make than you think. The chicken stock can be made early in the day, or another time and frozen. At dinner just bring stock to a boil and add the dumplings. **The finished broth should be rich in taste so I always cook my chicken in organic chicken broth instead of water.** *Combine the following ingredients, bring to a boil and continue cooking on medium heat for 1 to 1 ½ hours based on the size of the chicken.* **This is the best chicken stock you've ever tasted:**

-   *1 organic **rinsed** whole chicken. I have to be careful what words I use because I told my husband to **wash** a turkey once, and when I checked he had the turkey in the sink full of soap bubbles. Remove back and breast skin, the tail and other large fat deposits (leave skin on the wings and part of the legs for flavor). Put the neck in the stock; boil giblets up separately to eat or give to your animals.*

-   *Add 2 quarts of organic chicken broth (**I use the Imagine brand**).*

-   *1 stalk of **finely chopped** organic celery (taste to make sure it is not bitter).*

-   *2 cloves of **finely chopped** organic garlic or use the chopped garlic in jars.*

-   *10 organic baby carrots **finely chopped** (or one large carrot). I do not keep large carrots on hand because they may lose nutrients waiting to be used. Since I use the baby carrots in my salads, they stay fresher for all recipes.*

-   *1 medium organic **yellow** onion **finely chopped**. I use yellow onions here because you want strength of flavor, and not the sweetness of white or red onions.*

-   *½ tablespoon of organic dried parsley or 1 tablespoons of finely chopped fresh.*

-   *1 teaspoon of sea salt. Commercial salt developed a bad name because it is only sodium and chloride making it very imbalanced … and capable of producing disease. Totally balanced natural sea salt with all the trace minerals is a super food. **<u>Never buy sea salt</u>***

189

in open bins as the moisture evaporates and you lose the minerals. Besides Celtic sea salt another good brand is Redmond Sea Salt.

When the chicken is tender, remove it from the liquid with two spatulas onto a plate and separate the meat from the bones. Place ½ of the chicken back into the liquid, and save the other ½ for another meal (like a stir fry or sandwiches).

For a large family, you can make 1 ½ times the stock ingredients, and put all the chicken back into the liquid. *I keep this stock in the freezer all the time so it is ready to make quick meals on other days.*

DUMPLINGS

Mix the following ingredients for easy to make dumplings (½ recipe for 2-3 people).

- *2 cups of organic whole grain flour (spelt or quinoa makes a lighter dumpling than whole wheat).*
- *1 tablespoon of aluminum free baking powder plus ½ teaspoon natural sea salt.*
- *3 tablespoons of organic **soft butter** (measured carefully) cut in with a fork or pastry cutter. **Never use Better Butter as the added liquid makes the dumplings too soggy and you want the batter to be very stiff.***

*Drop rounded tablespoons onto **BOILING** stock and cook covered on medium heat about 10 minutes, turning once.* **Or, you can add cooked noodles.**

I serve dumplings and chicken in a soup bowl **with memories of Grandma's days.**

A fabulous salad completes the meal, and makes you a super cook …again!

THE WORLD'S HEALTHIEST LEGUMES

Legumes make up the category of food comprised of dried beans and the edible seeds that grow in the pods of plants. If you crack open a legume it will have a row of seeds inside it (thus beans and peas). **In the whole scope of blocking disease they are of great importance.** Legumes got a bad reputation as being the poor person's food … or they took a long time to prepare … or they produced gas. **There should be no excuse not to use legumes frequently with the organic canned beans so easy to fix either hot or cold.**

The following 5 varieties come out on top in terms of all-around nutrient quality and high fiber that will help your body stay strong and ward off disease:

1. **Lentils** – beat out all other legumes as **<u>number one</u>** for an impressive show of nutrition. Did you know that? Its history dates back 8,000 years. *Use organic canned lentils <u>that have been rinsed until all foam is gone,</u> with organic dried seasonings of choice like garlic, onions and sea salt. Put the heated mixture into an organic whole grain pita bread with fixings of your choice, like finely chopped organic white onions or Spring onions, organic mayonnaise, organic relish, organic sprouts, chopped lettuce, shredded Manchego sheep cheese, organic diced tomatoes or organic catsup … **need I say more … make it delicious! Enjoy new combinations in your pita bread … or add ingredients of choice to organic canned washed lentils and accompany any meal, or add to a salad.***

    Make soup:

    – *Cook 1 large red or yellow onion, 4 garlic cloves, and 1 stalk chopped celery (taste to make sure it is not bitter) in 2 tbsp. olive oil for 5 minutes.*
    – *Add 4 slices (or more if desired) cooked crumbled turkey bacon*
    – *Add 1 large can of organic canned tomatoes*
    – *Add 1 can of washed lentils (or bean of choice)*
    – *Add 2 cups Imagine brand chicken broth* **(no-chicken broth if chicken not tolerated)**
    – *Add 1 tsp. sea salt and 3 tbsp. organic Canola mayonnaise **that is the secret ingredient!** Simmer for 30 minutes … **enjoy!***

2. **Black Beans** – another legume with a massive nutrient wallop. An article in Food Chemistry and Toxicology emphasized the benefits of whole black beans on protecting DNA damage … something we really need help with in modern times. Most people have heard of black beans and rice but associate it with Mexican food. Black beans are so easy to fix with the organic canned black beans that are ready to go with only a rinsing to get rid of the foam. *Use them added to fresh chopped sweet white or red onions and organic Canola mayonnaise in salads, pita bread or as a side dish. Black beans make wonderful soup and you can stir canned and rinsed black beans into any cooked rice dish for added nutrition.*

3. **Dried Peas** – (includes split peas) do not need to be soaked before cooking, but may be a helpful added step for some people with poor digestion. You do not need to make Pea Soup to use this nutritious food. Add a few dried peas to any soup or casserole dish, even if the recipe does not call for it. ***Learn to be nutritiously creative!***

4. **Pinto Beans** – this bean looks like someone splattered it with paint, hence the name derived from the Spanish word for 'painted.' They are the most consumed dried bean in the U.S. and deserve the #4 spot because of a nutrient dense make-up. You can combine any choice of beans for a delicious 3 Bean Salad that is even better if made the day before. **Here are some <u>ingredient options</u> for 3 Bean Salad:**

   - *3 cans of **different** organic beans, thoroughly rinsed.*
   - *1 tablespoon of organic olive oil; sauté 5 minutes with 1 **medium** (not large) sweet **white or red** onion finely chopped, and 3 cloves of finely chopped organic garlic.*
   - *¼ cup (or less) of Coconut Vinegar sweetened with Coconut Crystals to taste and a little Stevia if you want it sweeter.*
   - *½ teaspoon each of organic dried oregano and basil. **ENJOY!***

5. **Lima Beans** – also known as butter beans, have amazing potential. They are nutritionally dense … and filling, so they help with overeating. They come from … guess where … Lima, Peru. Don't mess with a fancy recipe. You can rinse a can of organic lima beans; add sea salt and Better Butter for a creamy, nutritious taste treat! A study from Japan suggested that the lectins in lima beans may be helpful in cell regeneration. Eden Organic has canned Baby Lima Beans; if you cannot find them check www.edenfoods.com. You can also find organic baby lima beans in the freezer section of your health food store.

Other beans you can use with confidence are the white **Great Northern Beans** typically used for baked bean recipes. I never make the long version of baked beans anymore when I can get such a delicious, organic, canned version from Walnut Acres. *Their baked beans are sweetened with maple syrup. If directly out of the can is too sweet for you, add an extra can* *of organic rinsed and drained Great Northern Beans and adjust ingredients other than the sweeteners to taste. This stretches the beans for a large family.*

<u>Rinse all the foam off 3 cans of organic white beans to make this easy soup:</u>

1. *In 1 tablespoon olive oil, sauté 1 large organic chopped red or yellow onion, and 3 large organic garlic cloves.*

2. *Simmer 10 minutes with a large can of organic chopped tomatoes*

3. *Season with ½ teaspoon thyme (or 1 teaspoon fresh), 1 teaspoon basil (or 1 tablespoon fresh) and sea salt to taste.*

4. *Add the beans and 1 cup of organic Imagine brand chicken broth…or* **vegetarians can use vegetable broth.** *Cover and simmer 20 minutes.*

PANTRY/REFRIGERATOR SOUP

I love to make this soup when I get overstocked with vegetables. These soup recipes usually cannot be duplicated, but I have never made one that was not delicious, and I felt so good about cleaning up food instead of wasting it. **The next time you want to clean up some overstocked foods … think soup!**

We all need to eat more legumes, and now with the canned organic legumes available in most health food stores, eating legumes has never been easier. Remember 20 and 21 for other bean recipes. Work all the organic canned beans into your meal planning because EACH NUTRITIOUS BEAN IS A LITTLE PIECE OF HEAVEN!

AWESOME MEATLOAF

FROM DORI'S KITCHEN - 36

If you ever watched the TV show *Everybody Loves Raymond* you have heard all the jokes about bad meatloaf. Everyone should have a favorite meatloaf recipe. This light and delicious recipe feeds four people, but can be doubled for larger meals ... or a desire for an easy 2nd meal ... or leftovers for sandwiches. Buffalo is a red meat, and harder to digest unless you are hydrated with energized water and have a normal saliva pH, preferably 6.6-7.0. Mix together the following:

- *1 lb. of ground buffalo found in most health food stores that carry meat. You can also make meatloaf out of ground turkey, chicken, ostrich, or emu.*
- *½ cup of any non-dairy milk (preferable not soy due to high estrogen levels in many people).*
- *¼ cup of ground **sprouted** flaxseed. I never buy flaxseed already ground, or take flaxseed oil that can easily turn rancid. Ground **sprouted** flaxseed added to food or blender drinks is a super source of nutrients, essential fatty acids and fiber, easier to digest and does not go rancid like other flaxseed products.*
- *¼ cup of any organic tolerated bread (about ½ slice), toasted and crumbled into bread crumbs.*
- *⅓ cup of finely chopped organic **yellow** onions (you want a strong flavor here).*
- *⅓ cup of finely chopped organic celery (taste to make sure it is not bitter).*
- *1 medium (not large) beaten organic egg.*
- *½ tablespoon of Worchestershire sauce.*
- *2 whole finely chopped **large** organic garlic cloves or chopped garlic in a jar.*
- *½ teaspoon of natural sea salt (more or less to taste).*
- *½ teaspoon of organic ground thyme.*
- *⅛ cup of organic catsup spread over top before baking. If you cannot eat tomatoes try your favorite mustard over the top.*

Mix well, *and pat into a sprayed casserole dish to fit this recipe or double version. Spread catsup or mustard over the top of the loaf. Bake at 350 degrees for 1 hour, or 1 ½ hours if you double the recipe.*

If you bake sweet potatoes, red potatoes or squash, you should put them in the oven at 400 degrees for 30 minutes, and then lower the temperature to 350 degrees for the meatloaf. Meatloaf can be served at the table with optional freshly ground black pepper.

Black pepper can turn rancid, so always freshly grind when desired and never cook with it in the recipe. Cooked black pepper can have a toxic element that is hard on the liver. <u>Black pepper can also be a source of symptoms for people who cover most everything with pepper.</u>

If you do have any leftovers, you can heat the meatloaf in the oven **in a covered casserole** the 2nd night and make a hot meatloaf sandwich with slices of onion, lettuce, and whatever you want!

OR… your already cooked potatoes or squash the second night added to the meatloaf in a little Better Butter can be the base of a great quick stir fry. **OF COURSE … always add a fabulous salad to your meal!**

ENJOY … MAYBE EVEN 2 NIGHTS!

DO YOU LOVE WHITE POTATOES?

Most people love white potatoes. Americans eat more potatoes than any other vegetable. Children and adults alike may or may not eat a lot of vegetables, but give them potatoes and they clean their plate! Unfortunately potatoes do not have the vitamins and antioxidants most vegetables contribute to the diet. *So what DO potatoes have?* They are **high in starch** and that can send your blood sugar soaring after eating a serving of this favorite food. Potatoes have a high glycemic index (GI) which can contribute to a person gaining weight, or develop disorders such as pre-diabetes or diabetes. **<u>Potato belongs to the nightshade family of foods that may not be tolerated by people with joint disorders and chronic fatigue.</u>**

If deleted from the diet most people will miss white potatoes. <u>If you want to eat potatoes make them easier to digest red potatoes instead of white potatoes.</u> Organic sweet potatoes, sweet white turnips, parsnips and Jicama are not in the nightshade family and can be substituted in many recipes.

Cook organic frozen sweet potato fries according to directions. Another idea is to sauté but do not brown 2 tablespoons of minced garlic in 2 tablespoons olive oil. Add fresh or dried parsley and toss with baked sweet potatoes and natural sea salt to taste. **I order less chemical rice in a restaurant instead of potatoes because a commercial potato can have herbicides, pesticides, roundup, fungicide, mold retardant and sprout inhibitor.**

A new study, according to *Prescriptions for Healthy Living*, November 2005 article by James Balch, M.D. **suggests blunting the blood-sugar raising effect of high carbohydrate foods simply by adding vinegar to your meal.** *One to two tablespoons can be added to sauces, gravies, cooked meats, cooked vegetables and salad dressings. There are many varieties of vinegar.* White distilled or malt vinegar from grain can be a problem if you are gluten intolerant. Cider or wine vinegar can be a problem if you are sensitive to smoke, perfume, or may be hyperactive. Rice vinegar is generally tolerated and **my favorite** is Coconut Secret Vinegar. Here is Dr. Balch's salad dressing recipe:

DIJON VINAIGRETTE SALAD DRESSING

- ¼ cup of Balsamic vinegar … (or your most tolerated vinegar).
- 2-4 teaspoons of Dijon mustard.
- 1 teaspoon kosher salt (use sea salt); fresh ground black pepper optional
- ⅔-¾ cups of extra-virgin olive oil.

Note: optional recipe could simply be your favorite mustard and favorite vinegar sweetened with Stevia or Coconut Crystals.

ENJOY THIS LEMON DRESSING ON VEGETABLES OR RED POTATOES

Many people do not like certain vegetables like broccoli, cauliflower, green beans, asparagus, etc. because they are cooked until mushy and tasteless! Consider this…

- **Always** cook vegetables al dente … **never mushy.**
- **Always** cook organic vegetables … they just plain taste better without chemicals!
- **Always** add a dressing to the vegetable to **give it a spark!** You could use Better Butter and sea salt … but if the cooked vegetable is served with a starch in the meal like sweet potatoes or red potatoes, then warm this **vinegar dressing**:

Squeeze an organic lemon, add 1 tablespoon of your tolerated vinegar, 1 teaspoon of organic dried oregano, and ¼ cup of organic olive oil.

IF YOU HAVE TO ELIMINATE POTATOES CONSIDER THE FOODS THAT CAN BE AN ACCEPTABLE SUBSTITUTE IN RECIPES … AND ENJOY YOUR SWEET POTATOES.

FABULOUS STEW

Stews are **fabulous** to freeze for future meals, or a large family dinner, or hungry family or guests after an outing. VEGETARIANS CAN SUBSTITUTE BEANS FOR THE MEAT. It can be made ahead when you have more time and have delicious food ready when you need it. If you do not like lamb, you can substitute a whole organic chicken, 2 Cornish game hens, buffalo or deer meat. *I love a good organic lamb stew so this is a personal favorite.* Healthy stews and other chopped vegetable recipes are a snap with vegetable chopping equipment you can purchased from QVC Home Shopping Network.

To make a hearty stew base recipe, combine in a soup kettle:

- *4 large or 5 medium organic lamb shanks, or trim all the fat off of lamb shoulder chops for **part** of the meat, but the shank bones help flavor the broth; or a <u>skinned </u>whole chicken removing as much fat as possible; or skinned 2 Cornish game hens that are often tolerated by people allergic to chicken, or a piece of buffalo or deer meat that is naturally lean … or <u>organic rinsed canned beans for the vegetarian.</u>*
- *3 quarts of organic Imagine brand chicken broth or No-chicken broth.*
- *2 **very large** chopped organic celery stalks (taste to make sure they are not bitter).*
- *6 **large** chopped organic garlic cloves or chopped garlic in a jar.*
- *1 **very large** organic **yellow** onion for strength in taste (or 2 medium).*
- *1 bag of chopped organic baby carrots or you can use 6 scrubbed and chopped whole carrots.*
- *2 teaspoons of natural sea salt or add more to taste at the end of cooking.*
- *4 large or 8 small Bay leaves **that you remove after cooking before adding potatoes , mild white turnips (or the smallest regular turnips), or another potato substitute.***

*Simmer for several hours or until the meat falls off the bone and remove the meat from the broth. Separate the meat from any fat and bone and **store in the refrigerator until ready to add back later**. Skim most of the fat off by hand with a spoon or liquid baster and proceed with the recipe. **<u>When the fat is skimmed off add the meat back to the broth. At this point you can freeze some of the base recipe and continue with a portion for dinner.</u>***

1. *Scrub 4 large unpeeled organic red potatoes, cut out eyes and blemishes and cut into medium size cubes.* **You can also add a few white turnips or small regular turnips, but large turnips can be bitter and strong tasting ... or consider a potato substitute from 33.**

2. *Add to the stew along with 1 tablespoon of organic dried parsley or 2 tablespoon of chopped organic fresh parsley.*

3. *Add 1 teaspoon each of organic basil, marjoram, thyme and rosemary. <u>If you add the herbs before you skim off the fat, you will pull them off with the fat.</u> Bring to a boil and simmer about 30 minutes until ingredients are done. Adjust seasoning according to taste.*

ENJOY ... once you've tried this hearty and healthy stew, you will want to double or triple the base recipe and freeze for future quick meals. When you are tired and rushed all you need to do is to get the base recipe out in the morning to thaw, and at dinner just add the herbs and your choice of red potatoes, turnips, a potato substitute or rice.

This stew meal is complete except for one of your prize winning salad.

AWESOME MACARONI SALAD

FROM DORI'S KITCHEN – 39

This recipe is an exercise in creativity and individuality. You take a list of ingredients and make it suit *YOUR* taste, *YOUR* protein choice, or make it vegetarian. **This salad is delicious, nutritious and picture perfect!** How much of each ingredient depends on the amount of macaroni you cook, so I'll list the ingredients and you can decide how much you need to make it taste just right.

The best macaroni is the organic brown rice penne pasta from Tinkyada sold in many health food stores, or call 1-888-323-2388. This pasta cooks and tastes like wheat pasta and is wheat and gluten free. The whole package says it serves 6 people, but by the time you add all the ingredients it will serve 8 people. Cook in salted water, rinse and drain. While the pasta is cooking you can cut up the following, or use a vegetable chopper you may have purchased.

– *1st choice should be finely chopped organic* **white or red** *onions (not strong tasting yellow onions). The amount of onion is based on your love of onion flavor. If you only like a mild onion flavor use white onions or the white part of Spring onions, and a little of the green part.*

– *Amount desired of finely chopped red, yellow or green peppers.*

– *Amount desired of finely chopped celery, yellow and green summer squash that have all been taste tested to make sure they do not taste bitter. Adding bitter tasting vegetables can ruin a macaroni salad.*

– *Amount desired of finely chopped radishes.*

– *You can also add some of the white part of Bok Choy that is very mild and adds more crunch ... or consider raw slivered Jicama for crunch.*

AND NOW THE SAUCE ... THE FIRST 3 'SECRET INGREDIENTS' MAKE ALL THE DIFFERENCE!

- *Drain the pasta, and in the same pan melt about 4 rounded tablespoons of Better Butter (recipe on 29) if you cooked the whole package of pasta.*

- *Add organic Imagine brand chicken broth or (**No-Chicken broth for vegetarians**) based on the amount of pasta and the desired moisture content.*

- *Add 4-8 tablespoons of organic Canola mayonnaise based on the amount of pasta. When you finish the recipe you should not have dry macaroni, but should have a little extra sauce to make it a <u>slightly juicy</u> finished recipe. Adjust the chicken or No-Chicken broth and mayonnaise to make the finished recipe as moist and flavorful as you like.*

- *Generously sprinkle with organic garlic powder that I like better in this recipe because you get the garlic flavor without the raw garlic breathe, or a strong bite of garlic here and there.*

- *Generously sprinkle with organic dried parsley or chopped organic fresh parsley if you chop it VERY FINE.*

- *An optional addition is sliced black olives.*

- *Put the cooked, rinsed, and drained pasta into the mixture.*

- *In your freezer you should have your container of a stock mixture of organic sunflower seeds, organic pumpkin seeds and organic pine nuts. Sprinkle over pasta and mix thoroughly. The seed mixture makes it a complete meal. You can also add a few sesame seeds or poppy seeds.*

- *The finishing touch of color is cherry tomatoes cut in half that can be mixed throughout or layered over the top for a more dramatic presentation.*

This is a great dish to consider if you are asked to contribute to a pot luck luncheon or dinner. Macaroni salad may be made the evening before, or early in the day before an event because flavors seem to marinate together when it sits awhile. <u>Make sure it is in a tightly sealed container so the salad does not pick up a refrigerator taste</u>. QVC has some wonderful locking portable containers perfect for transporting to an event.

For some hearty eaters wanting more, or a desire to make a very dramatic luncheon or patio presentation for guests or cold summer supper, consider the following options added to your macaroni salad:

- *Cook per directions the raw ecologically raised medium shrimp. Place macaroni salad in the middle of the plate and spread the shrimp around the outside. You can offer an organic* seafood dip available in most health food stores. Also consider adding cooked salad shrimp to the recipe.

- Make Deviled Eggs by hard boiling eggs according to the instructions on 12, then cut in half lengthwise and scoop out the yellow part into a small bowl. Add organic Canola mayonnaise, organic relish and natural sea salt to taste. Fill the egg shells, sprinkle the top with paprika and place around the pasta.

- Purchase any smoked fish, cut into small pieces and place on a whole grain organic cracker around the pasta.

- Mix a can Wild Planet Albacore, Skipjack tuna or salmon, or sardines in water with organic Canola mayonnaise, organic relish and natural sea salt to taste. Place on a whole grain organic cracker, and place around the pasta if it will be eaten soon as the moisture will soften the cracker. You can always serve the mixture in the middle of a separate plate with crackers around the edge.

- Macaroni salad can be served warm or cold, and can be an addition to any soup recipe that you may already have in your freezer from my other recipes.

- Arrange on a plate and top with leaves of artichoke hearts in a pattern with cherry tomatoes in the middle for a flower effect. You can also make a flower design out of strips of black olives and cherry tomatoes in the middle.

- For a special summer party presentation hollow out a ripe pineapple or half of a watermelon and fill with the macaroni salad. Serve the pineapple or watermelon cubes with toothpicks as a side dish.

Now just serve and accept the compliments!

BEAN STEW

FROM DORI'S KITCHEN — 40

If you are tired of thinking chicken all the time ... try turkey. This recipe is delicious with a hormone and antibiotic free turkey breast you can buy in the health food store. You could substitute ostrich or emu, but some people do not realize you can sometimes buy turkey parts without buying a whole turkey. ***You can also adjust this to be a vegetarian stew.*** Put this together for rave reviews:

- *Cut turkey or chicken breast, ostrich, or emu into small bite size pieces, and place in a slow cooker. <u>Everyone should own a slow cooker because it is so easy to throw a few ingredients into it in the morning, and dinner becomes very quick to fix.</u> You could stir-fry this recipe but that has to be done at dinner time when the family situation may be more hectic. With a slow cooker your dinner is almost done when the household gets busy.*
- *2 cups of organic Imagine brand chicken broth. Only use 1 cup if you stir-fry and use No-chicken broth for a vegetarian stew.*
- *2 tablespoons of organic olive oil.*
- *1 very large white, red, or yellow sliced organic onion. White onion gives a very sweet flavor, red less sweet and yellow onion a stronger flavor.*
- *2 large organic diced garlic cloves, or 1 teaspoon of organic powdered garlic*
- *1 medium stalk of organic celery sliced and tasted to make sure it is not bitter.*
- *1 teaspoon natural sea salt or more to taste.*
- *1 tablespoon of organic dried parsley, or 2 tablespoons of fresh parsley.*
- *¼ teaspoon each of thyme, oregano, marjoram and basil ... or more to taste. You can experiment with other herbs or fresh herbs if you grow your own.*

You can cook this part of the recipe for 6 hours in the slow cooker on low setting. If the meat is cut into small pieces, it takes about 1 hour as a stir-fry. This is a simple stir-fry if you make it a vegetarian stew.

<u>Add the following to heat thoroughly, but do not overcook:</u>

- *Organic green and/or yellow zucchini cut into strips ... amount as desired to add quantity for extra servings. Always taste zucchini before adding to a recipe as some can be bitter and it could ruin the recipe. For at least part of the winter you may not be able to get organic yellow zucchini, but green zucchini is usually available. Small zucchini are less likely to be bitter than the large size.*

— *Rinse 1 can of organic Great Northern beans or any organic canned bean of choice under running water until ALL FOAM IS GONE. This is a delicate recipe so the milder beans like Pinto or Great Northern works best. Add as much as you like to the recipe … and if any is left over you can use it the next night on a salad. Beans make great filler if you want to stretch a recipe.*

This recipe has some sauce to it, so it is best served in a soup bowl.

A great salad makes it an easy meal that should get you 2 thumbs up!

NUTRITIONAL BLENDER DRINK

FROM DORI'S KITCHEN – 41

THIS DRINK IS FULL OF MULTIPLE NUTRITIONAL FOODS THAT MAKES 2 MEAL REPLACEMENTS OF SUPERIOR QUALITY AND IS EASY TO DIGEST AND ABSORB. THE DRINK MAKES ONE QUART DIVIDED INTO BREAKFAST AND LUNCH; OR BREAKFAST, LUNCH, AND DINNER; OR SIPPED ALL DAY IF YOU ARE ILL OR HAVE POOR DIGESTION. <u>THE DRINK HELPS REST THE DIGESTIVE SYSTEM SO IT STARTS IMPROVING HEALTH AS THE LIQUID DRINK DOES NOT NEED THE DIGESTIVE SYSTEM TO BREAK DOWN THE FOOD.</u> ANYONE WITH A URINE OR SALIVA pH BELOW 6.6 WOULD BENEFIT FROM AN EASY TO DIGEST LIQUID BLENDER DRINK.

THE FOLLOWING INGREDIENTS ARE BASIC <u>OPTIONS</u> TO THE DRINK. YOU CAN PICK THE ONES YOU LIKE OR CAN TOLERATE. THERE IS NO SELECTION THAT MUST BE IN THE DRINK EXCEPT THE WATER BASE:

- *16 OUNCES OF FILTERED ENERGIZED WATER* **(PART OF YOUR DAILY WATER).** If your urine or saliva pH is below 6.6 you can add ½-1 cup of 100% pure coconut water to the drink that is balancing and hydrating. Coconut water was used during World War II for blood plasma and is a perfect choice for a body out of balance.

- *2 TABLESPOONS OF SEED MIXTURE* YOU **KEEP IN THE FREEZER** THAT CONTAINS SUNFLOWER SEEDS, AND PUMPKIN SEEDS. If you have problems with nausea eliminate nuts and seeds due to high fat content and add later when your symptoms improve.

- *1 TABLESPOONS OF ORGANIC SESAME SEEDS* THAT LOWERS BLOOD SUGAR. Hulled sesame seeds may be easier to digest than unhulled. Unhulled contains more fiber but added fiber may not be needed in this drink that has plenty of fiber.

- *¼ CUP OF QUINOA FLAKES (FOR ONE MEAL DRINK) OR ⅓ CUP (FOR A*

TWO MEAL DRINK) FOUND IN THE CEREAL SECTION OF A HEALTH FOOD STORE IS LOW GLYCEMIC INDEX COMPLETE EASY TO DIGEST PROTEIN AND ALKALINE. Quinoa can be put into drink without cooking.

– *1 TABLESPOON OF TEFF FLOUR* ADDS PROTEIN, FIBER, IRON AND IS GLUTEN FREE. Teff flour also thickens the drink so it is more like a meal instead of thin water.

– *2 TABLESPOONS OF* **SPROUTED** *FLAXSEED (REFRIGERATE AFTER OPENING).* Flaxseed that is not sprouted is hard to digest so always use organic sprouted flaxseed.

– *1 SCOOP DAIRY FREE, SOY FREE, AND SUGAR FREE PROTEIN POWDER.* ONE EXAMPLE IS RAINBOW LIGHT RICE PROTEIN POWDER SWEETENED WITH STEVIA. **OR,** TRY 1 PACK OF GREENS PAK OR REDS PAK. All choices are available in many health food stores or www.amazon.com. In my opinion the best combination is one Greens Pak that is your nutritional base and one Red Pak that is the antioxidants you need to survive living in modern America.

AFTER INGREDIENTS ARE ADDED TO BLENDER, FILL TO 32 OUNCES WITH MORE WATER OR ANY OF THE FOLLOWING CHOICES:

– *ORGANIC ORIGINAL RICE MILK, CAROB RICE MILK (OR ADD CAROB POWDER TO DRINK FOR EXTRA CALCIUM), CHOCOLATE RICE MILK IF CAFFEINE TOLERATED, OR HAZELNUT MILK. IF UNSWEETENED IS RECOMMENDED FOR YOUR DIET USE UNSWEETENED ALMOND OR HEMP MILK.*

– *CONSIDER IMAGINE BRAND BUTTERNUT SQUASH SOUP. **ALL CHOICES COUNT AS PART OF YOUR WATER.***

CONSIDER ADDING ANY OF THE FOLLOWING:

– *1 TEASPOON MACA POWDER THAT IS AN ADAPTOGEN TO HELP WITH STRESS AND GLANDULAR HEALTH.* This is available in most health food stores.

– *IF TOLERATED 2 BRAZIL NUTS (FOR ANTICANCER SELENIUM), 2 FILBERTS, 2 WALNUTS AND 2 PECANS ARE ACIDIC NUTS; 4 RAW CASHEWS, 4 ALMONDS ARE ALKALINE NUTS.* All nuts may be considered for mid-morning or mid-afternoon snacks instead of adding to the blender. **KEEP ALL NUTS AND SEEDS IN THE FREEZER AND BUY ORGANIC.**

–   *BEETMAX IS A LIVING FOOD THAT IS ONE OF THE THREE BEST FOODS FOR THE LIVER (THE OTHER TWO ARE OLIVE AND LEMON).* I recommend 1-2 teaspoons in your drink for added nutrition; it makes the drink taste good and a pretty pink color. If you cannot find it order from Hallelujah Acres 1-800-915-9355 or www.hacres.com.

THE FOLLOWING INGREDIENTS SWEETEN YOUR DRINK IF ALLOWED IN YOUR DIET PROGRAM:

–   *CONSIDER 1 SERVING OF ANY STRONG FLAVORED FRESH CITRUS, BERRIES, OR FRUIT OF CHOICE GROWN IN THIS COUNTRY.* All American grown fruits are low in fructose and therefore less stress on the digestive system and the liver.

NOTE: TROPICAL FRUITS LIKE BANANA, PAPAYA, MANGO AND PINEAPPLE OR ANY FRUIT JUICE, CORN OR CANE SUGAR, OR HONEY ARE HIGH IN FRUCTOSE AND CONTRIBUTE TO BELLY FAT AND FATTY LIVER SO ARE NOT RECOMMENDED IN A DAILY BLENDER DRINK.

THE FOLLOWING SWEETENERS ARE ALLOWED IN ALL DIETS (EVEN DIABETICS) AND HELP TO MAKE THE DRINK TASTE ENJOYABLE:

–   *LOW GLYCEMIC AND FRUCTOSE FREE ORGANIC STEVIA*
–   *OR COCONUT SECRET CRYSTALS.*

For some people the blender drink is the best way to improve health. For others too busy to eat correctly the blender drink is a gift of convenience. If you make a drink and do not like it you should not give up on this idea, but try other ingredients and change the recipe until you do like it. If you make a drink and feel nauseated you may have to omit nuts and seeds until your DIGESTION improves. The effort will be rewarded in improved health!!!

Enjoy ... you are worth it!

BEANS AND RICE

Look for opportunities to use beans … <u>any beans fixed any way!</u> This is a basic beans and rice recipe, but you can change it in a lot of ways. The basic ingredient is organic canned beans. *Rinse them thoroughly to get off all the foam that is the indigestible sugar that causes intestinal gas.* You will generally get less intestinal gas from organic canned beans then beans you cook from scratch. Put together the following ingredients to feed 3 people, or 2 people with a left over lunch the next day:

- *Put 2 tablespoons of olive oil in a skillet with a lid.*
- *Add 1 large organic chopped white, red, or yellow onion.*
- *Add ½ cup of chopped organic celery. Taste first to make sure it is not bitter.*
- *Add 3 large cloves of chopped organic garlic … or if you are in a hurry you can use 2 teaspoons of organic garlic powder or chopped garlic in a jar.*
- *Add ½ teaspoon **each** of thyme, oregano, and basil.*
- *Add 1 very large or several small bay leaves **that you remove before eating.***
- *Add 1 cup of any organic rice (I prefer organic brown Basmati or Jasmine rice).*
- *Add 2 cups of organic Imagine brand chicken broth … or you can vary the taste with organic vegetable broth, or organic vegetable juice to make it vegetarian.*
- *An **optional** addition is a 14 oz can of diced tomatoes. **Make this recipe one time with a tomato base, and another time <u>without</u> any tomatoes for an entirely different taste.***
- *Add 1 teaspoon of natural sea salt (or to taste).*
- ***Now here is the creative part.** The last time I made this I added chopped ostrich steak strips. Ostrich tastes like beef in a recipe. You can also use raw chopped chicken or turkey breast meat … or **keep it vegetarian.***

Cook on medium heat until the rice is soft (about 40 minutes). You can now clean up the kitchen, set the table and make the salad. If you have family help, this is a good time to call them (my husband makes award winning salads). To finish the recipe, add …

- *½ cup of organic chopped green pepper, and cook covered for about 5 minutes more. The green pepper tastes best if it is not cooked soft.*

— *Remove bay leaves, and at this point you can add optional spices depending on how seasoned you want it to be. A more Creole version of this recipe may include optional spices like cayenne pepper, chile powder, hot pepper sauce (health food stores have many versions of this), cumin or freshly ground black pepper* **always added just before eating.**

— *1 can of <u>thoroughly rinsed</u> organic Kidney Beans … or you can use Pinto … or Black Beans. You have all heard of Black Beans and Rice, but fold the black beans in gently at the very last or the rice will look black if the beans get mushy.*

Serve this with the super salad you already made. <u>If you make extra you can put it in a taco shell the next night for a really quick meal.</u> You've fixed a great nutritious meal, and because of your organizational skills the after-dinner clean up will be easy.

Take your deserved credits …you are so smart!

GRILLED FISH AND VEGETABLES

Get out your George Forman grill for delicious and quick ideas. You can use any fresh or thawed frozen **firm** ocean fish. Check www.realsimple.com/fishguide for fish low in mercury. I prefer frozen because that fish was usually frozen on the ship, or soon after. Fresh fish may not be as fresh as you think, so be sure you can trust the store. **The out of date sticker should not be today or tomorrow's date.** Due to some deterioration of the fish in transport, the best fish is frozen right on the fishing boats within hours of being caught. Other selections are frozen at plants as soon as the iced fish is brought in from the boats. **I never buy store fresh fish unless it was put in the case that day … so always ask!** I often trust frozen over what could be 'so called' fresh. Look for wild, pure, all natural, or vacuum-packed, type of information on the packaging of the frozen fish you consider. **<u>Always cook fresh fish the day it is purchased.</u>**

Be willing to learn about the difference in fish. For example, swordfish is firm, meaty and high in protein … it is considered the sirloin of the sea and is the best choice for kebabs. Swordfish can be high in mercury, so only eat occasionally. Sole is extremely soft, and is best in a sauce where you can scoop it out with a spatula. Make a decision to go down the fish list and try different choices with different sauces … YOU WILL FIND SOME FAVORITES YOU WILL WANT TO MAKE OVER AND OVER!

Fixing grilled fish is as easy as picking a sauce. There are many listed in the Nutrition Chapter of my book The Power to Heal. Change the sauce and you have created a different meal. You can use any organic salad dressing you like, or make your own with **<u>any of these options</u>** that you can also use to grill the vegetables first:

- *¼ stick of organic butter, or Better Butter (recipe on 29).*
- *2 tablespoons of olive oil if you do not use Better Butter that contains oil.*
- *½ tablespoon of Balsamic Vinegar or Coconut Secret Vinegar… (or if you cannot tolerate vinegar try lemon or lime juice).*
- *1 teaspoon of any enjoyed mustard.*
- *1 teaspoon of organic garlic powder, garlic paste or chopped garlic in a jar … or fresh garlic if you have it.*

- *½ teaspoon of basil.*
- *½ tablespoon dried parsley … or fresh if you have it.*
- *After the vegetables are grilled and kept warm in the oven, **before** you put the fish on the grill add 1 teaspoon of dill **or** ginger to the leftover sauce.*

ADJUST INGREDIENTS AS DESIRED AND TRY THIS BLENDER SAUCE

- *4 ounces of organic Santa Cruz bottled lemon juice.*
- *½ large organic red chopped onion.*
- *2 large organic chopped garlic cloves.*
- *2 teaspoons of organic honey … or sweeten with Stevia Coconut Secret Crystals or Coconut Nectar if you are reducing or eliminating fructose.*
- *½ teaspoon of natural sea salt, and ⅛ teaspoon of dill.*
- *12 ounces (1 ½ cups) of filtered water.*
- *Mix in a blender until smooth … **adjust taste** … and spoon over grilled fish.*

Before you grill the fish, grill the vegetables as described on 7. Even asparagus can be grilled (*You can also coat asparagus with salt and olive oil and broil for 8-10 minutes until tender*). Coat each piece with your favorite salad dressing, or try the suggestions above. Use the drip pan, and as the juices drip down pour them back over the vegetables a few times until they are done. This makes them extremely tasty and moist. As you pour the sauce back over the vegetables it will start to run off the edge of the grill, so when you remove the drip pan to re-marinate the vegetables, replace it immediately with another drip pan or you will have a mess on the counter. My George Forman Grill came with 2 drip pans.

When the vegetables are grilled and kept warm in an oven at 200 degrees, spread the sauce of choice on the fish pieces, and grill based on thickness and denseness. A one inch thick slice will be done in 4 minutes; dense swordfish may take 7 minutes.

If you choose not to grill vegetables, you can:

1. *steam vegetables like green beans seasoned with salt to taste, 2 tablespoons olive oil, ½ cup **roasted unsalted** choice of chopped nuts, and ¼ cup organic dried cranberries.*

2. *serve with a simple salad of mixed greens tossed with chopped artichokes, 3 tablespoons lemon juice and ⅓ cup of olive oil.*

3. *steam broccoli and toss with 6 cloves sliced garlic cooked until golden in ¼ cup olive oil, 2 tablespoons lemon juice, ½ cup lightly toasted chopped hazelnuts.*

4. *serve with a vegetable plate of assorted raw vegetables.*

Grilled fish served with grilled vegetables, or a simple single vegetable is a year round

family favorite … or fabulous enough for company! Don't forget that quinoa is a fabulous, nutritious, easy to digest alternative to rice with any meal!!! Just substitute the quinoa for the rice and fix the same.

TRY THESE FAST FISH RECIPES WITHOUT GRILLING

- *For a real fast meal, boil fish in seasoned water with sea salt, garlic powder, dried onion and dried parsley for 20 minutes. Lift out and serve covered with any organic chutney of your choice from the health food store.*

- *Try simple boiled or broiled fish served on a bed of whipped sweet potatoes with one of the vegetable suggestions above.*

- *Try simple boiled or broiled fish with all the fixings for a fish sandwich.*

- *Sauté, lightly salted mahi-mahi in 2 tablespoons of olive oil about 5 minutes to a side. Place on a bed of mixed salad greens with 1 ripe avocado cut into strips. Drizzle a sauce over the top made with 1 teaspoon olive oil, 2 tablespoons lime juice, and 2 teaspoons of Coconut Secret Nectar. Top with 2 Spring onions <u>very thinly sliced length way</u>. **<u>This makes a beautiful family or company dinner presentation!</u>***

- *Heat oven to 400 degrees. Rub cod filets cut into 2 inch **bite size pieces** with olive oil and sea salt. Roll each bite size piece of fish in **crushed** organic corn flakes and place on a sprayed baking dish. Bake 15-20 minutes depending on the thickness. Serve with your favorite dipping sauce, and a great salad.*

- *Blend ⅓ cup of pecans or walnuts, the thinnest shaving of a lemon or 1 teaspoon of organic lemon juice, 3 large garlic cloves, ⅓ cup of quinoa flakes and ½ teaspoon sea salt in a small food processor. Coat 1 pound of any mild white fish fillet with the mixture and lay on an oiled casserole. Bake for 20 minutes at 400 degrees or until the nuts are toasted brown. Drizzle with more fresh lemon and serve with your favorite salad and a cooked vegetable.*

- *If you gave up tuna because of the mercury fix your favorite tuna recipe with Wild Planet Skipjack tuna that is low in mercury and in a BPA free can.*

- *If you stopped buying fresh salmon because of the cost you might find Wild Planet BPA free canned salmon is affordable. Make your favorite salmon patty recipe or fix like you would tuna fish salad.*

SEAFOOD DOES NOT HAVE TO BE COMPLICATED TO FIX

You can make a simple shrimp or crab chowder with the following ingredients:

- *Sauté ½ cup each of chopped carrots and onions plus ¼ cup celery (make sure it is not bitter celery) in 1 tablespoon of olive oil until vegetables are tender.*
- *Stir in 2 tablespoons quinoa or spelt flour and 2 teaspoons fresh thyme (or 1 teaspoon dried).*
- *Add 2 cups organic chicken or vegetable broth.*
- *Add 1 pound of peeled and deveined shrimp or crab meat and simmer no more than 5 minutes.*
- *Stir in ⅓ cup of coconut milk (not lite coconut milk) and heat only to warm. <u>If you like a richer chowder you can use less broth and more coconut milk to make 2 and ⅓ cups of total liquid.</u>*

A big bowl of steamed mussels and a fabulous salad makes an easy meal!

If you do not feel well on store steamed shrimp it could be the MSG in the seasoning. You can ask the store to steam the shrimp without any seasoning while you finish your shopping. Bring the steamed shrimp home and ask a family member to help you with cleaning and deveining. While the shrimp is being prepared you can collect your favorite vegetables and make a fabulous shrimp (or crab) salad. This is especially a good suggestion for the hot summer. Be creative with the vegetables and consider adding easy to fix Deviled eggs on the side if you have some hard boiled eggs in the refrigerator. Top the creation with your favorite salad dressing and Tara chips for crunch.

GOOOOOOOD EATING!

FISH STICKS, PASTA AND QUINOA SALADS

FISH STICKS MADE AT HOME

Prepared fish sticks are often too expensive for some budgets especially if you need multiple packages for a family, or the product may contain ingredients you cannot tolerate. *It can be frustrating to find one ingredient you should not eat listed on something you want. Here is a way to make baked breaded fish at home easy and less expensive.*

1. Preheat oven to 350 degrees.

2. *Purchase 4 cod or any other firm fish appropriate for fish sticks and cut into thick strips. **Always buy fish that came in that day.** Mix together:*

   - *1 tablespoon organic dried onion flakes.*
   - *2 chopped organic garlic cloves or 1 teaspoon of organic powdered garlic.*
   - *2 tablespoons of organic Santa Cruz bottled lemon juice available in health food stores.*
   - *¼ teaspoon of sea salt (more or less based on preference).*
   - *½ teaspoon thyme … or other herb of choice.*
   - *2 tablespoons of melted organic butter (not Better Butter because of the liquid). <u>Coat fish in mixture on both sides.</u>*

3. *<u>Then coat fish</u> in ¾ cup of tolerated organic whole grain bread crumbs. Choose either wheat, spelt, rice or millet you can either buy if available in health food stores … or toast and blend your tolerated bread choice in a blender until fine.*

4. *Place on a sprayed pan and bake uncovered for 30 minutes, or until the bread crumbs are crisp and brown. When serving, top with your homemade seafood sauce mixing Spectrum Canola mayonnaise with organic pickle relish. Fish sticks are also good drizzled with Coconut Aminos.*

5. *<u>Serve with a super salad, or this pasta salad:</u>*

PASTA VINAIGRETTE WITH ARTICHOKE HEARTS

1. *Toast ¼ cup of pecan or walnut pieces in a 350 degree oven for 10 minutes, and set aside.*

2. *Cook 4 ounces of your choice of pasta shape – from angel hair to macaroni.*

3. *Combine 3 tablespoons of olive oil, ¼ cup of Balsamic vinegar or Coconut Secret Vinegar, 1 crushed organic garlic clove, ½ teaspoon of basil, ½ teaspoon of natural sea salt (or adjust to taste) … toss with rinsed and drained pasta.*

4. *Add 1 can of artichoke hearts cut into small pieces (not the marinated kind). Artichokes are intimidating and some people go a lifetime without trying one, but canned artichoke hearts are easy to use and add nutrition and taste to salads. Optional addition to the recipe is ½ cup of sliced mushrooms if you do not have a mold allergy.*

5. *Add 2 tablespoons of fresh finely chopped organic parsley, ½ cup of halved organic cherry tomatoes and the toasted nuts. **TOSS FOR A BEAUTIFUL SALAD!***

DO NOT FORGET ABOUT QUINOA FOR EASY TO DIGEST PROTEIN

Quinoa stands alone as gluten free, easy to digest <u>complete protein</u> grain. The best protein you can consume if you suspect digestive problems or are chronically ill. Quinoa flakes are perfect in blender drinks. Quinoa flour can be used anytime gluten free flour works … like in coating meat or fish, thickening sauces, pancakes or waffles. Quinoa seeds cook up like rice and can be a protein staple in many recipes.

This is a good salad for any meal short of protein, or protein for a vegetarian:

1. *Cook 2 cups quinoa per directions, drain and let cool spread out on a cookie sheet.*

2. *Toss with ½ cup crushed **toasted** hazelnuts or any nut of choice, ¼ cup minced green onions, ¼ cup dried organic cranberries that have been soaked in warm water and drained, ¼ cup olive oil, 2 tablespoons of a tolerated vinegar and natural sea salt to taste.*

EATING HEALTHY HAS NEVER BEEN SO EASY!

ADDITIONAL IDEAS FOR BASIC INGREDIENTS

We have come through an incredible journey together … getting in touch with your best potential … and learning to eat healthy food without thinking it takes hours in the kitchen to prepare. This is the last idea … *sob* … and rather than another recipe you will learn about some basic ingredients that you can make …whatever! **The trick to cooking is being able to know what products work together … what are some SECRET INGREDIENT tricks … and how willing are you to STRETCH out of your culinary mold and try new things.**

BASIC INGREDIENTS … AND OPTIONS THAT HELP ANY RECIPE

1. Any sauce can start out by softening chopped organic onions and garlic in olive oil. Use white or red onions for a mild flavor, Spring onions for even milder flavor, and yellow onions for a strong flavor. Use organic powdered garlic if you are too rushed to chop garlic.

2. Do not be afraid to use herbs. *I keep my organic dried herbs on the refrigerator door to help them stay fresh and reduce mold growth.* I put dried or fresh parsley in almost every recipe because it is good for digestion. Use basil if you want to sweeten the recipe. Equal amounts of rosemary, thyme, and marjoram seem to work well together anytime. Use this combination to flavor any plain brown rice that you cook with organic chicken or vegetable broth instead of water. *If you have a window ledge, you can have an herb garden!*

3. Cayenne, chili powder, or dry mustard adds a 'kick.' **Freshly ground** black pepper should be added at the table, **NEVER COOKED IN THE FOOD!** Do not forget about dill and lemon juice on fish.

4. Organic Imagine brand chicken or No-chicken broth, other vegetable broth of choice, non-dairy milk and clam juice should be **stock** items to add liquid to any recipe and give more flavor than water. Add organic tomato juice to change the flavor of an old recipe.

219

5. I use coconut milk or organic Canola mayonnaise for any recipe I want to be creamy. Spectrum Canola mayonnaise mimics sour cream in any recipe. Canola gets a lot of bad press but unless you make your own egg free mayonnaise from the website recipe, in my opinion, Spectrum brand of Canola mayonnaise is better for you than soy mayonnaise for the occasional mayonnaise requirement. You can avoid other sources of Canola like oil. Coconut milk gives a sweet taste.

6. If a recipe needs 'something' try a little Balsamic Vinegar or Coconut Vinegar to give it a boost, or Spectrum Canola mayonnaise. ***Raw Coconut Aminos*** *is a soy-free vegan seasoning sauce that is 100% organic, gluten and dairy free. The raw coconut sap is blended with sun dried sea salt and is very low glycemic. The minerals, vitamins, nearly neutral pH, and 2-14 times the amino acid content of soy makes it a super food that is absolutely delicious as an added sauce to anything without a coconut flavor.* ***If you cannot find it call 888-369-3393.***

7. This trick gives the recipe 'energy.' Anytime you make a stir-fry, just before serving, add slices of red tomato, or cherry tomatoes cut in half, or slices of red or green peppers and slices of black olives to the stir-fry to heat BUT NOT TO COOK. This adds drama and energy, and makes everyone say ... ohhhhhhh that looks so pretty!

8. Any dull salad can take on new life by adding pumpkin or sunflower seeds you store in the freezer and Terra Exotic Vegetable Stix (or crumble the chips) for color. Crunch can save a salad or a recipe, so do not forget about the unusual vegetables discussed on 33.

9. Crumbled organic turkey bacon can add flavor to recipes and vegetables.

10. Keep organic hard boiled eggs on hand that can help in many ways at the last minute. Do not forget to make Deviled Eggs occasionally ... your family will love you for it.

11. Keep both olive oil and another mild pan spray on hand. Sometimes you want to spray a pan, but do not want the olive oil flavor.

12. Always have Better Butter made for everyday use that stays soft in the refrigerator, has essential fatty acids, and is high in Vitamin A and Vitamin D. Also have some spare butter in the freezer because sometimes a recipe cannot handle the liquid in Better Butter.

13. Some oils you thought were bad ... are not. Avoid all foods with trans-fats or partially hydrogenated oil. Some tropical oils contain saturated fats, but are not all bad.

    –   Coconut oil and coconut milk are both stable and do not become rancid even when stored a long time. When oils spoil they contribute to disease. Mary Enig, PhD, one of the world's experts on fats and oils, said, "There is no downside to consuming natural coconut oil, and there are many benefits." Coconut milk now comes in a 'lite' version for that perfect pumpkin pie and curry sauces.

– Palm oil and palm kernel oil are not the same. Palm oil comes from crushing the **fruit** that is boiled, and the oil then rises to the top in a safe way to extract the oil. Palm oil is ½ saturated and ½ unsaturated fat used throughout Europe and Japan. Palm kernel oil is a by-product extracted from the **seeds or nuts** of the tree, and is less desirable because it is higher is saturated fat, and may contain chemicals used as solvents. If you use Palm kernel oil, it should say 'expeller pressed.'

– Sesame oil should not be over looked because it can help lower blood sugar. I use sesame oil whenever possible. I use sesame seeds on salads, in blender drinks and in many recipes. Toasted sesame seeds in Better Butter can save a plain vegetable.

14. If you have trouble finding a salad dressing without troublesome ingredients, make your own. If you cannot handle grain or apple cider vinegar buy rice vinegar or Coconut Secret Vinegar and add to organic olive oil. Once you experiment with ingredients and find a salad dressing you like to make at home, it can be used for more than salads … marinate fish, meat, fowl or grilled vegetables.

15. If you are gluten intolerant you can try the rice and corn pastas. Also, buckwheat is not a grain but has a gluten-like protein that may or may not be tolerated by people intolerant to gluten. It is worth a try if your gluten intolerance is **mild**, because Eden Selected 100% whole buckwheat pasta (Buckwheat Soba) is delicious.

Note: If you do not have time to cook there are many organic meal selections in health food stores that are healthier than 'fast' food. If you do not want to heat up your large oven, buy a small toaster oven … but **DO NOT MICROWAVE! YOU DO NOT WANT TO DESTROY THE NUTRIENTS IN YOUR GOOD ORGANIC FOOD!**

To my new culinary friend, I wish you enjoyment in the kitchen because like life, cooking should be interesting and creative … and NEVER boring! Hardly a month goes by that someone does not say, "I did not think I would ever eat that, but now it is a part of my regular diet." **So … forget the mindset of yesterday and be open minded to new tastes and healthier choices.**

BE THANKFUL FOR THE FOOD THAT KEEPS YOU HEALTHY. LEARN TO EAT TO LIVE INSTEAD OF LIVING TO EAT AND MAKE EVERY RECIPE … YOUR RECIPE!

**LET YOUR KITCHEN CELEBRATE YOUR CREATIVY …
AND SUPPORT YOUR WELLNESS!!!**

ABOUT THE AUTHOR

THE PERSONAL HEALTH SUCCESS STORY:

Dori Luneski, R.N., N.D. was chronically ill for twenty years, struggling with poor health on all levels of mental, emotional, and physical. She became so ill she was often bedridden and the quality of life was gone. Life itself became a challenge in survival. Finally, she found doctors who treated the CAUSE of illness instead of just the symptoms. She learned the 'laws' of wellness and experienced an incredible metamorphosis. The cocoon of a sickly body became a healthy, vital person. Now at 78, people meeting her for the first time marvel at her vitality, energy and enthusiasm.

THE PROFESSIONAL:

Dori has been a leader in the health field for over 50 years, both in traditional medicine and holistic health. Past career work that has contributed to her holistic view of wellness includes two prevention oriented health clinics for 12 years, a rehabilitation nurse for four years, a psychiatric nurse for 6 years, plus three years of personal development seminars, numerous holistic health seminars, and two years of Homeopathic classes. That background, her Naturopathic Doctor diploma, and 18 years as a Naturopathic Practitioner gives her insight into all aspects of wellness and stress management.

THE SPEAKER:

Dori is trained by the National Speakers Association. She is a one-stop source of information on all levels of spiritual, mental, emotional and physical. Her credits include teaching wellness in seminars, courses, conventions, radio shows, television, newspaper articles, teleconference calls and lectures for a variety of audiences.